Seasons & Crossroads
vol. 33
of

The Poet's Domain

Copyright March 2020, Hampton Roads, Virginia
Wider Perspectives Publishing – J. Scott Wilson

Poetry and Writings herein are products of the authors listed with those works and all rights to those works revert to the authors at the time of 2nd run/release of this volume. Authors are therefor responsible for distribution and withholding of their works after such time and should be contacted for permission before any repackaging, reproduction, or recirculating of their pieces. Permission granted by one author does not translate to permissions over any other authors' works and the individual authors shall have final control in resubmitting their own work beyond this volume to contests or other anthologies after March of 2020.

If you are unable to order this book from your local bookseller, then please contact the publisher directly.
HRACandWPP@outlook.com

With immense appreciation to Pat Adler & Live Wire Press, and to the Poetry Society of Virginia.

The Poet's Domain
Vol. 33 copyright Hampton Roads, Va. Feb.2020
Seasons & Crossroads
1st ed. ISBN: 9798608479595
2nd ed. May 2020 ISBN: 978-1-952773-99-0

The Poet's Domain

Seasons & Crossroads
volume 33

A Collection of Poems

compiled and edited by J. Scott Wilson

Wider Perspectives Publishing

March 2020, Hampton Roads, Virginia

More than a dedication…

To Patricia A. Adler, longtime contributor, co-editor and sometimes sole editor of The Poet's Domain. She tirelessly worked to promote poetry scribblers from within and around Virginia into the ranks of published authors -- either through their contributions among pages just like these or into volumes of their own works.

In that way, she was a supporter of those poets. She was also ready to acknowledge those who supported her along the way. In the months right before her November 23, 2019 passing after brave battles against cancer, I carried out the regrettable duty of informing Pat of the loss of Nancy Powell. Her mind went immediately to the weight of losing someone who had been so supportive of her work and that of others. In the summer of 2019, a couple of years after her announced retirement to attend to the coming health struggles, Pat had busied herself in the task of getting just a few more poets with significant projects out into print – just a few more.

She was not the first to edit or publish The Poet's Domain, but she took the reins for quite a while and did a great deal with it – all good – and it is my hope that I do her legacy and trust justice in keeping it going forward.

Particia Anna was born into the Strehl family in March of 1938 and she left this world via Mechanicsville, Va in November 2019. Those surviving her; ex-husband turned friend, 3 sons James, William, and Christopher, 2 grand-children and a brother can surely attest to the world being better having had her. So can a couple hundred poets.

Talented artist, poet & healer

who sought truth, light & love

Contents

S.A. Borders-Shoemaker	The Winter-Spring	1
Barbara Brady	Winter Walk	2
Alisha Brown	Is There an Emoji for That?	4
Jason Brown	Crossroads	7
Jack Callan	Constitutional Quandry	8
	Fools of August	10
Joan Casey	Every So Often	11
	Family Free	12
	It Was the Season	13
	Rehanging the Bird-Cage Chime	14
	Risk	15
Norma Cofresi	Red Betta	16
	Transitions	17
	A Visitor Passing Through	19
Karen Cummings	I'm Stuck	20
	My Baby	21
Sharon Dorsey	The Desk	22
	Happiness Sits Softly	24
Anne Emerson	Birdsong	26
	Late Fall	27
	Past and Future	28
Serena Fusek	The Center Does Not Hold	29
	Change of Season	30
	Opens the Sky	31

(Serena Fusek, cont.)	Tuesday Afternoon	33
	Yes, Like a Song	35
Amanda Gregory	Breaking the Cycle	37
	Fly Baby Fly	38
Linda Griffin	Getting Through Cancer	39
Doris Gwaltney	You Know It	40
G. Barry Hamann	Air	41
	I Have Beheld My Own Awakening	42
	Journey	44
	A Trail of Fire	45
Jan Hoffman	Autumn Reflections	46
	Come Before Winter	48
	Patient in 3021-B	49
	Wilmington, Vermont, 2008	50
Shari Leigh	Crossroads	51
	Seasons & Crossroads Haiku	53
Terra Leigh	December	55
	New Wine	56
Ed Lull	Ben and Agnes	57
	Blessed Journey	60
	Night ~Villanelle~	62
Crickyt J. Expression	Mirage to Oasis	63
	Musing On How I've Changed	64
Linda Partee	A Sestina For Mother Nature	65
	A Spring Canvas	67
	Winter's Cusp	68
	Young Bride	69

Author	Title	Page
Lucy Quinn	'Til Death Us Do Part	70
Robert Rickard	At Home on Poros	72
	The Certain Spring	74
	My Library	76
	Sacrifice	78
Dawn Riddle	Etchings	80
	Until	81
Kailyn Sasso	Inverno	82
	Wilted	84
Ann Shalaski	Departure	85
	Just So You Know	86
	Pedal Past Perfect	87
	A Simple Song	89
Barbara Drucker Smith	Autumn of Our Lives	90
Karen Sparrow	Old Black Train	91
	Saying Hello	92
	The Seasons Cycle	93
Judith Stevens	Avian Christianity	96
	Remembered Taste of Blackberries	97
Ken Sutton	Black River	99
	Coffee in the DMZ	100
	Maps & Photographs	103
	Sgt. Mitchell's Visit	106
Tammy Tillotson	Bells Ring	109
	Cost of Living	111
	Travellers	113

12 Keys	Another Letter to God	114
	I am Not Broken	116
	Seasonal Change	117
Jack Underhill	Cold Morning Unfolding	118
	Embraced by Fall's First Blush of Cold	120
	Floating Feathers in Late Spring	122
Charles Wilson	'56 Pickup	123
	Family Plot	124
	How to be an Artist	125
	Jukebox	126
	People are Different at Saying Goodbye	127
J. Scott Wilson	Aderezo	128
	Eleven Hours on the Ferry	130
	First Days of Winter	132
	Hydroplane	133
	Real Ironic Hobby;Trainwatching	135
Henriann Woleben	Winter Season	136
Gus M. Woodward II	Seasons Have Their Reasons	137
Rabbi Israel Zoberman	Beyond	138
	Migrant Ishmael	139
	The Irish Jewish Museum	140
	The Pond at Birkenau	141

Contributor's Award	143
Meet the Poets…	144
Foreword	154

The Winter-Spring

S.A. Borders-Shoemaker
Smithfield, Va.

Sundry feathers and pearls of frost
    wrap and cross her body
like a funerary and birth procession
that carries across earthen glass.

Hair and pine
intertwine and weave
signs of youth and age
crowned beneath effervescent gossamer.

Glass turns under toe to soil
soil turns to stone
and stone yields to sand
down by the altar of the river.

Sacrifice for chance
at the crossroads of history
and anticipation
brings the bride to the rushes.

First the skirts
then the bodice
teem to immerse
in rime and seasonal change.

One breath
two, three
fog becomes light
and feathers in water slide free.

The marriage, complete
of holly and hoarfrost
heralds to the flowers lost
to feel again.

Winter Walk
For Sean

Barbara Brady
Burgess, Va.

The pale, barefaced beach sleeps,
too lonely and cold to notice
my dog Sean and me coming down
its storm weathered steps.

We hesitate at the last rung,
before Sean bounds to the sand,
his copper coat fluffed in excitement,
his soft brown eyes smiling.

I tramp behind in my worn Wellies,
green monsters crunching hard
sand into big, foot-shaped prints
of frigid, unyielding crust.

Bundled in thoughts of warmth,
I plod and push along,
holding Sean's leash at long lengths,
struggling against his pulling.

Come On, his eyes say, dancing,
fancying each beach offering,
joyfully engaged in the simple,
artful act of sniffing.

Driftwood the color of old snow,
scatters along this timeless strand,
like deep wrinkles on ancient parchment,
talismans of another time.

Withered pampas plumes quiver,
in the freezing fingers of wind,
too gentle to resist, too strong to give way,
awaiting the long song of death.

A bald Eagle fresh from nesting
sets her massive wings windward,
gliding over silver waters,
a soaring speck on the pearl horizon.

Slap size waves frozen mid-roll,
hug the shore in a collar of frost,
far off tides scroll slush
over iced water, sighing.

Sean stops and looks seaward,
Summer memories swimming
blithely beneath his Irish brow,
beckoning the child within his soul.

He jumps and twirls on long legs,
begging for the Bay. "No," I say,
this water's chilly silly boy,
not today, not today!"

The ivory sun streaks behind dark
Southern pines, pointing our way home.
We pause, not wanting this walk to end,
our eyes searching for tiny signs of Spring.

Not yet, the wind whispers, stinging
the beach with winter breath. Not yet.

Is There an Emoji for That?

Alisha Brown, Norfolk, Va.

I do not speak emoji,
just as my parents
did not speak computer.
I fear the day
when I send a
colon parenthesis :)
to my child
and they look at me
like I am the wrong species,
not fit
for this technological life.

*"Do not let Mom
wander online alone."*

Perhaps they will simply
shackle me
with old technology.
Slow,
so Mom can keep up
in her emoji-less state.
Poor handicapped mother,
sending people random eggplants,
thinking its
just a funny vegetable.

They will plan their teenage
assignations in emojis
letting me see everything,
knowing I understand nothing.

I wonder if they
will have an app for that,
translating emoji to me
and cursive to them?
Written languages
standing on either side
of the generational divide.

Perhaps I will use cursive
to plan my elderly hookups
in the old folk's home.
Carefully writing

eggplant

in a flowing script,
slipping to the guy
who can still see,
hoping he
will slip *it* back to me.

I forgot
he's too old,
to speak emoji.
Now he thinks I'm
one eggplant short
of a fruitcake.

Do they have
an emoji for that?

The Poet's Domain

> I return to squinting
> at my Emoji to English dictionary,
> large print edition,
> while I peck out a text
> to my granddaughter.
>
> The hearts are easy to find.
> After all,
> love transcends all divides.
> And yes,
> they have an emoji for that.

Jason Brown
Dark Mtr
Virginia Beach, Va.

Crossroads

The lease is a prison sentence
   At this point
Stuck in an unfortunate now
Now or never
Decision to sever
From this endeavor
Poor sleep
Demons in the mug
 anxiety laden nightmares
My cup runneth over with
Feelings of anger
Now I feel like a stranger
Despite my house key
What was once a misunderstanding
Is now the undying
Need for release
I believe I'm at a crossroads
You've scared off my beloved
Left a ghost in my bedroom
Room mates can leave a home feeling like a doomed place
Do I grit my teeth for six months
Or clear my savings account
And get my shoes laced

Jack Callan
Norfolk, Va.

Constitutional Quandary

   Children of immigrants,
        children of slaves,
my country 'tis of thee, down to our graves.
       We hold tight these truths,
even if you didn't believe them
        when you wrote them down, Mr. Madison.
We will hold you to it,
      'til we can improve your work -
but take your "master's" hand
       off the power of this pen,
'cause your heart was darkened and dirty
      when you wrote it down. Amen.

Buyin' an' sellin' human beings,
      then breakin' 'em into his ground -
would trade 'em for books
          to help improve his philosophy.

Didn't help a damn thing, far as we see,
       jus' dragged his man around
          'til he learned 'bout freedom in Philadelphia -
could never take him back to Virginia
     'cause after that, he knew too much
an' he would tell the other slaves – no, suh, couldn't have it.
An' our someday president, Master Washington,
        an' his "Book of Negroes"
helped catch 'em when they run away.
         Now seize your property, Mister 'tis of thee,
           hunt 'em down from sea to sea,
    choke on your cry for liberty.

Needed to sell his man to buy books,
        an' complainin' of the difficulty.
O', say can you see
    can't see the hypocrisy.

Go ahead, write your Constitution
      with its house of cards divided
          countin' person and property.
You're outta' three-fifths of your mind.
           Constitution jes' a cracker barrel
              if it ain't go no soul.
It just run us all into
      this rotten ol' hole,
         an' so far,
    we jes' stuck.

Jack Callan

Fools of August
for Jim Holden

The toil of God's curse
        is the city hot day sun, a hundred and
any fool with a gun could blow it open.

Gonna' be a sopper, a show-stopper,
        a sweatin' be like blood sucker.
Las' thing out is mud and light'nin' – almost fright'nin' -
        lot o' it pourin' down, be so strikin'
                me not to die, why?
Light'nin' boys do fancy duo do, do dance,
        do the tango, like a strange oh, a sorry two
                with sparks alight
                      on smokin' grey beards.

You got'ta cut that bag o' rock an' dust –
        then dump it, mix it up, while the scribbled
fiddled live wire like 'Merica
        where animals and children lie in cages
                      and cry.

See two crazies workin'
        like they wanna' die, sweet by and by,
like dumb come with maturity,
        an' I can't stop 'til it's over
'cause ain't no one but us
            too old to fuss an' dumb be enough
                to jes' get it done
        and don't die – why?

            Find out later.

Joan Casey
Newport
News, Va.

Every So Often

They said it was a once in ninety-year snowfall
but in his ninety-three years
he had never seen the mountains so white

and the limbs and trunks of naked trees
outlining dozens of ridges
he never knew were there.

Patches of fallen sun shone on the road,
bushes in the valley glittered
like a Christmas card he got one year.

Winter had finally come, but it was already spring,
time to plant spinach seed,
       then again maybe not.

Joan Casey

Family Tree

Rooted in our senses
we see, hear, feel, smell
sensations our trunk and limbs carry
to our crowns for thought.

In one way we are the whole tree,
and at the same time,
just a leaf
like on a family tree.

One wonders about the architect of archetypes –
why the use of such few simple symbols
to haunt us into significance,
teach us language even beyond words,

give us a place on a branch
of life that has a season
whose reason
is to give birth to tomorrow.

Joan Casey

It Was the Season

when leaves go silent
garden empties
of birds at the feeder
sun darts in and out of cloud
like us
wondering whether to leave
or stay.

No amount of planning
takes away fear of fallen limbs
days of wet on your breath
water at your feet
nights of no light
with time
to just wait

for the wind
and rain to get tired,
for more time
to wonder whether to leave
or stay
or have something to do
besides waiting for the season

with no crossroads
       to end.

Rehanging the Bird-Cage Chime

Joan Casey

I am at the stage of life I once could never imagine,
now it's a day less and less far away.

I traveled time filling spaces
with pictures of smiling faces.

I wove flowers on a satin dress,
bought silver to stick in my ears.

I was a fierce hunter on black Fridays,
ferreting and fretting about what I thought was wanted.

Now I want someone to want what I can't throw away
and to let me keep forever what I can't hold in my hands.

I rifle through dented and dusty boxes and find
everything but the consumer's guide I faithfully followed.

With your love in my hands, I rehang
      the bird-cage chime for one more day.

Joan Casey

Risk

It draws me in like a cave

whose black mouth
invites discovery

of amorphous mists,
seductive fog horn
hinting at secrets

of closed doors,
unmarked envelopes,
wrapped boxes,
unopened dreams.

I tremble
with excitement,
shudder dreams might end,
take a deep breath,
begin.

Red Betta

*Norma Cofresi
Williamsburg Va.*

Through my mother's protracted illness,
my sister took care of her.
Sometime before my mother died,
my sister brought home
a Red Betta Fighting Fish.
She called her Lola La Colará
Puerto Rican for Lola the Redhead.

Lola lived in a fishbowl on
the white Formica kitchen counter
by turmeric-colored pill containers
covered with white, childproof caps.
When the sun hit the counter,
the pill bottles filtered orange light
as Lola's red color flickered
from orange to a deep golden yellow.

Time passed, Lola still lived,
but she was slower,
her skin, fins, and tail were straggly
and her once luscious color dimmed.
When I visited, I'd ask, Is Lola still alive?
My sister would look away and say,
She is doing all right.

In the few days,
it took our mother to die,
I lost sight of Lola.
I did not have the heart
to ask my sister when Lola died?
My best guess is that
Lola is with my mother
gilded by the sun's golden light.

Norma Cofresi

Transitions

I cross the veil between
life and dreams,
not re-hashing victories.
Each fault and imperfection magnified.

Hopscotch squares each a mystery
peopled by the past's forgotten ghosts.
Each room a theatre set to play
humiliations, failures, the implausible.

I almost catch your smiling scent
whispering a love song
disappointed neurons turn off
to stumble awake alone.

Night beats on as the clock
ticks guilty memories, one after the other.
A weary mind spins my age-trampled body,
My exhausted mind whirls with the dead of night.

A tired dance of crumpled sheets
of quiet prayers, of broken dreams.
Grasping and hoarding wide-awake hours,
not really knowing what death will bring.

I'm sandwiched between early morning darkness
and the approaching dawn with
blinking lights and whirring sounds,
indifferent harbingers of death.

I am not afraid to die
but of waking up to withered limbs,
nutrients and oxygen pumped into
tubes attached to unwilling flesh.

Tethered still to the in-between
I drift away like a balloon.
A wish fulfilled,
the unknown welcomes me.

A Visitor Passing Through

Norma Cofresi

Morning's cornucopia of chemicals just booted in.
Pain blinks in and out of awareness
toggled throughout the brain.
One of the voices in my head predominates:
breathe in, relax, give it time,
turn it on, turn it off.
As if I could.
Slipping through a crack between
the blackened sky and the purple beach
a sliver of pink announces the dawn.
I slide beyond the deceptive edge of sensation and pain.
And welcome the temporary emergence of comfort.

Karen Cummings
Norfolk, Va.

I'm Stuck

I miss you but you'll never know. My heart wants to love you endlessly, but my mind tells me to keep my distance. Stuck at a crossroads with my heart and my mind. Griping on to my insecurities like a security blanket, I suffocate in it. Wrapped around my fears, doubts, and past pain. These insecurities become my body suit of armor that I'm trapped in. And any thought of you and I being together gets pushed back from reality. I tell myself I'll never be hurt again, tears rushing down my face, as I breathe in more hurt from the past. My armor feels heavy, my movements become small. In the center of my chest plate is a stone brick wall surrounding my heart. As painful memories get stuck in a loop hole inside my mind, I can't let shit go.

Karen Cummings

My Baby

Would you have my mother's face, my grandmother's heart, my dad's courage, or my voice? Maybe; just maybe all the good in me I know would be you. I spoke about you to my sister as the tears cascade down my face like tidal waves crashing into one another. It took my breath away to say I had you and then I lost you. By now, you would've been in that awkward preteen stage, not quite a child, but not yet a woman. I can only imagine what life would be like through your eyes. It was too soon to know. Would you have been a courageous fighter, an outspoken activist, a daring scientist, or a thought-provoking teacher? October is pregnancy and infant loss awareness month, but my awareness of losing you is felt every day. Years ago, I had you in my stomach for a brief moment, and even till this day I still fall asleep holding onto my stomach. While thinking of you, I wake up to my hands still in that same position. I know God makes no mistakes, and for whatever reason, you weren't ready to come into this world. But please know your existence is felt for a lifetime. I never knew what you looked like, or sounded like, but I know you were mine and I love you.

Sharon Dorsey
Williamsburg,
Va.

The Desk

The roll-top looms large and intimidating in the small,
sunny room. My husband, Don, saved everything.
The endless minutia of life oozes from every orifice.
I have avoided this painfully personal treasure trove
for months, too traumatized by his death to tackle it.

Today, I dive in, starting with boxes beneath the desk...

...Military records going back to 1949, the beginning
of a 31-year career in the Air Force, culminating in
his promotion to Colonel in 1968 and retirement in
1980.
I watch him age in the
promotion photos,
wondering if I would have liked that stern officer.

...Divorce records from the early 80's,
attached to a neatly printed and numbered note,
listing the pro's and con's of ending a marriage.
The pro's won.
The marriage ended.

...An envelope, entitled, old friends and old flames,
filled with photos of smiling couples, skiing, hiking,
kayaking, against backdrops from around the world,
Don looking relaxed, happy, in all of them, not the
stern colonel, but the charming man I met in 1988.

...More papers financials from the purchase
of our dream house, our first home together;
a much-lamented speeding ticket for going
45 in a 35-mile zone, his first ticket ever, unusual
for someone who built and raced cars in his youth.

I sort the stacks into Save, Shred, Recycle, and Toss.
Then I tackle the drawers...

... Post cards of our trips to Mexico, Hawaii, British
Virgin Islands, and road trips to all fifty states,
a mini travelogue of our twenty-five years together.

... Glasses, magnifiers, hearing aids he refused to
wear,
love letters from children, from me, a welcome
to the world note for a new grandchild, scrawled on
an envelope.

... Cartoons, irreverent jokes, his favorite saying,
Life's uncertain. Eat your dessert first,
printed in big letters on a yellow paper napkin.

The sun is sinking low in the sky and shadows fill
the room as I wearily open the last drawer...

... Medical records, a year of tests, oncology visits, blood
transfusions, aimed at controlling a relentless enemy,
spawned by exposure to Agent Orange in Vietnam.

The desk is empty now, the messy, overflowing piles
neatly contained. Task complete – like the messy,
overflowing, uncontained life, also now complete.

As I stand up to turn out the light, a sticky note
flutters to the floor. In Don's handwriting it says,
I wouldn't trade tomorrow for the best yesterday
I ever lived.

Hard to lose a man like that.

Sharon Dorsey

Happiness Sits Softly

Happiness is like a butterfly,
the more you chase it, the more it will elude you.
Turn your thoughts to other things.
It comes and sits softly on your shoulder.

At 10, happiness was tangible – a shiny, new bike,
'til I saw my friend's bike had a pink basket and mine didn't.

At 20, happiness was a shiny, new husband,
'til he became a soldier and went to Korea for a long year.

At 30, happiness was a shiny new dream house,
'til dreams were shattered and the house was left behind.

At 40, happiness was children and family life,
'til infidelity reared its' ugly head

At 50, happiness reappeared, in the form of a new soul mate.
I nurtured it, hoping it wouldn't fly away.

At 60, happiness was a home together.
I thanked the universe every night.

At 70, happiness was replaced by her alter ego, pain.
Death marched into Happy Valley,
leaving behind fear and destruction.
I wondered if life's pieces could be glued back together.

Happiness crept back, after a time, not as shiny, still elusive,
a Meadow Lark's song at dusk,
a grandchild's laughter,
a peaceful heart.

Like the butterfly on a summer day,
happiness sits softly on my shoulder.

Anne Emerson
Williamsburg, Va.

Birdsong

Eve's treetops fill with chatter
like summer's cricket-cries.
Will birds so gather, always,
when longer daylight dies?

Or clutter onto branches
whose leaves adorn my lawn?
Or soar and fall like stardust
that will be gone by morn?

Anne Emerson

Late Fall

A tawny glow still shimmers from tall limbs
where fall's last gold defies tomorrow's ire.
It's past the date when treetops' color dims—
this year the season's burned a longer fire.
A frost can steal the brights or they'll be felled
by sobbing rains and gales; dank earth their bier.
But when, as now, for days good weather's held,
a ling'ring finery will reappear,
to shine as do my own reviving hopes
(not yet soft spring's suffusing promises),
like lanterns holding joy above the gropes
of sorrow's dour and wintry fruitlessness—
to be the engine of life's light renewed
at first relaxing of a bleaker mood.

Anne Emerson

Past and Future

It's late in March. The changing seasons fuse—
stark winter and new promise are as one:
some trees are bare, some misted with strange hues;
a chilly wind defies the blinding sun.
But soon enough, 'mid veils of bloom and green,
invading Spring will chase the frost away
from shadows, hollows where its starch is seen,
till seeds leap forth and soft new saplings sway.

In me as in the seasons one can see
tomorrow hovering with yesterday.
The last desires of youth are leaving me,
while early age begins its fruitful stay.
Now I am forty, past and future blend,
as spring and winter fuse at March's end.

The Center Does Not Hold

Serena Fusek
Newport News, Va.

Rain streams
from the swollen sky

drags the last leaves
into the street

where their colors dim
go out. Down the wet road

veiled by the torrent
someone wrapped

in darkness
(a black coat or

black wings) appears
or maybe a hole

opens in the day
where the center

has collapsed. All warmth
seeps into gray

drains down the sewers
with the gurgle
of autumn's rain.

Serena Fusek

Change of Season

"Spring!" declares
the calendar
and she grabs her broom,
marches through every room
attacking winter.

She sweeps up webs
and dead spiders.
She sweeps out dust bunnies
large enough to challenge
her fifteen pound cat.
She sweeps seed
spilled when she filled feeders
that sustained the birds
through icy weather.

Christmas glitter
dried mud from winter rains
leaf crumble in corners
bunch in front of the bristles.
She scoops   bags   seals
then grooms the broom.
The house gleams.

Now she opens windows
throws wide the door:
"Begone winter!"

and March scampers in
bringing a flurry of petals
that scurry across
shining floors.

Serena Fusek

Opens the Sky

Trees surrender green
don scarlet
gold amber   bright
as festival clothes

brilliance that passes
beneath the wings
of hawks   robins
riding winds
that sweep away
summer's haze

polish the air
until it shines
like new wine
opens the sky
like a present.

Like a stream
that freshly gushes
after August drought
the old yearning
surges through me.

A flood of monarchs
coverges for flight.
Tiny hummingbirds follow
the pole star's path.

A skein of geese
streams across heaven

    calling

        calling...

        I hear them calling
my name.

Serena Fusek

Tuesday Afternoon Around 3 PM

They were suppose to meet—
it was written in the stars (or so the fortune teller said.)
But she got caught in traffic which made her late
and she hurried past the bookstore
did not stop inside.

They were supposed to meet and, as a result,
he was supposed to die.

Instead, a year after they didn't,
on a Tuesday afternoon around three p. m.,
he passed a customer a latte and counted out change.
When the customer walked away
he was already five minutes
past the time he should have died.

He took the rag and wiped the counter
moving almost in a dance
while inside his bones and his untormented heart
something recalibrated.

He stood behind the counter and looked at the people
drinking their coffees and lattes and frappucinos
browsing magazines, reading books, peering at laptops.
A couple sat holding hands.
It seemed to him that her hands imprisoned the man's.

A man stepped to the counter. "Coffee. A grande please."
The new customer's hair was white.
Lines rayed around his eyes.

"Grande, yes sir!"
but it was habit that spoke and habit the drew the order.
Inside he was thinking "Some day my hair will be white."
Something was spreading through him, like a flush.

He felt it widen his eyes – he could feel the muscles pull
around the sockets.
It was astonishment.

Somehow white hair had never seemed an option before.

He blinked. He raised his eyes
looked beyond the muted light of the coffeeshop
to the bright, colorful bookstore. Then beyond the store
out the front window where
sunlight made the street radiant.

Serena Fusek

Yes Like a Song

The man who says yes
loves the sound
of a door opening.

The man who says yes
slides his tongue
through the last letter
while his mind turns over possibilities
as someone turns over earth
looking for treasure
or for nightcrawlers to bait
grandfather trout
from the river's depths.

The man who says yes
raises his gaze
to the mountain
and his mouth in a smile.

This man says yes
like it was a song
to which he knows
only the first notes
while he listens deeply
for the full chorus.

The man who says yes
stands at the threshold
stands at the top of the trail
stands at the crossroad--
steps forward

knowing the important decision
is not which path to take
but to choose to move.

The man who says yes
echoes the serpent's hiss
that lost Adam the walled garden
gave him all creation.

Amanda Gregory
Virginia Beach Va.

Breaking the Cycle

I'm falling for you again
I didn't think this could happen
I thought I was done with this love cycle
Why do you keep appearing on my path?
Why after I say no does spirit show me all these things
                                    that remind me of you?

Your name, whatever it may be, it's like you haunt me.
You show up in my dreams.

I'm not playing these games anymore.
I'm not falling for this trap where I am going to
        move forward with something when I'm not sure.

You will not confuse me because I am
                                not falling for you again.

Fly Baby Fly

Amanda Gregory

When we let go of needing to know
We trust in the unknown
Everything will be revealed to us in the divine timing of life
Sometimes we aren't the space to receive the answers that
                                                  we are so desiring

Stay open
Let go
Trust yourself and honor your true intentions
Be intentional with your time
The most sacred gift in this life
You are worth it all
Don't ever forget you are Gods child
The universe is here to support your path
Lean in and loosen the reigns that you are death griping onto
                                                             for dear life

Stop choke-holding your light
See your divine essence in those eyes

Seasons & Crossroads

Linda Griffin
Norfolk, Va.

Getting Through Cancer

Cancer does not possess me
Although it may invade my body
It cannot take away the zeal
Life can bring with compassion

I will not allow its consumption
To rule into useless thoughts
Bringing down the spirit of peace
Into anxious fears of dread

Encourage the disheartened
Help them seek their way
Their struggle is worth winning
Despite hardships along the way

Why must this I be subjected?
Useless fears' rule of my spirit
I know of no other way
But to subject myself to ruination

Mindsets of "I cannot do this"
Need to be shown that I can
Only through patience and love
Persistence and perseverance.

You Know It

*Doris Gwaltney
Smithfield, Va.*

Crossroads are what they say they are,
Roads that cross.
Seasons change them,
make them different
from the one they were before.
In all seasons there is change.
Road that make dry treads,
make muddy tracks.
Roads piled high with autumn leaves,
Pesky pieces of cut holly,
ready to bite.
All the countryside can offer,
But still they mesh,
they cross,
they bend.

G. Barry
Poquoson, Va.

Air

Air
Cool upon my skin
The breeze of a content
Autumn Day

Sweet smells of salted water
Interflowing with the spoils of Summer
As they find their way to the wet ground
From where we all began

Leaves that endured the late storms
Begin falling quietly as if they know it's
Time to let go
Returning home

G. Barry

I Have Beheld My Own Awakening

I have beheld my own awakening
As the words begin to flow
As effortlessly as melted snow
Guided by a force it cannot deny
My path directed by all I encounter
Never stopped but simply altered

My penned-hand flows onto the page
Pouring words upon words upon words
Channeled like the water by unseen forces
To the gathering pool of memories
And reflections of a life well lived
Mysteriously deep, dark and cool

I have looked into my own eyes
And seen what I do not recognize
Beyond what even the mirror can reflect
A truth beyond truth
The beginning of me from nothing
Nothing at all

You will know my words
Even if you do not know me
For I was and perhaps
I will be again
I am the snow melted to the stream
To the river to the ocean

I am again the snow
As white as the page
Below these imprinted words
Fresh and pure
Accepting of what is to be
From nothing at all

G. Barry

Journey

Journey
Thought to step
which divides
Is it up to me
Or the seasons of time
An artist's brush
An artist's guide
Back into darkness
And forward into light

G. Barry

A Trail of Fire

A trail of fire
Yellow-orange
To where my
Thoughts go
And where I cannot
Though my heart
Fills with possibilities
I'm lost of breath
At the beauty of it all
Fall

Autumn Reflections

Jan Hoffman
Williamsburg
Va.

It's an Indian summer evening,
so tonight, my mind wanders
back to the '50s and to an autumn
childhood where old morning glory
vines wrapped their dry arms
around rotted posts, and dry milkweed
pods, waiting for fairies to ferry them
off somewhere, drooped over the rusted
wire of a neighbor's sagging fence.

I'd sway on the plank of my tree swing
and marvel at the season's bruised fruit
—apples, peaches, pears—
that hid among tall blades of grass,
overgrown and neglected in the yard
of the abandoned house bordering
our backyard, its empty rooms
and attic havens for field mice
and families of scurrying squirrels.

Clotheslines and wooden clothespins
grasped shirts and sheets that
waved in the October breeze.
Frost glazed over excess pumpkins,
bright red four-o'clocks faded
into the dull brown of fallen leaves
of oaks and maples, and at night,
I watched constellations spin overhead
by the light of the smoky moon.

Tonight, I harvest memories
of those soft, hazy dreams
that followed the annual equinox
of my childhood, when brilliant
colors muted themselves, and studies
of Columbus were happy days,
when town roads had fewer potholes,
streetlamps dimmed each evening,
and concrete angels never haunted.

Jan Hoffman

Come Before Winter
for Tommy

"Do thy diligence to come before winter,"
Apostle Paul wrote his beloved protégé.
He was aging and ill and longed
to see his surrogate son one last time.

You are aging and ill, cancer spreading
and running wild like foul water
on those ancient Roman streets. Radiation,
chemo, and surgery have failed you so far.

We have no old record telling us if
the young Timothy ever made it to his
fading mentor in time, if he walked
or sailed or rode on worn beast to Rome.

I must leave Virginia and drive back home
to Indiana to embrace you this Christmas,
my brother, to see you eye-to-eye once more.
I must come before winter.

Jan Hoffman

Patient in 3021-B

In the deep purple of late twilight,
winter fills the room. She measures
the moments of her life—
inch by inch, year by year,
decades of coming, going, doing.

A chill causes her to shiver
as she replays actions, inactions,
desires, loss, detachment.
The cold of the bluish blackness
produces another shudder

as her shawl drops to the floor.
Her family gathers around
kissing final farewells,
not knowing she hears them
as she gazes into another realm.

Jan Hoffman

Wilmington, Vermont 2008

Early spring, we drive through snow
on dirt roads, and to our delight, we
check off a bucket list item: We see

metal pails strapped to maples. Steam
rises from local sugar houses. A man
invites us to watch sap boil, golden brown,

and then a woman on a short stool smiles
at us and funnels syrup into small glass
jugs with caps. We visit the 1836 Country

Store in the sleepy village in the valley,
the one with an American flag waving
outside in the courtyard. Glass cases

line the walls as we walk across uneven
wooden floorboards. Open shelves
offer jars of goodies: maple candy,

homemade fudge, slo-pokes, sugar daddies,
jawbreakers, red hots; all sorts of gum—
clove, black jack, bayberry.

We linger and stay longer than planned,
then stroll back outside onto cobbled steps.
Slow twilight arrives too quickly.

Shari Leigh
Norfolk, Va.

Crossroads

Just yesterday I was a mere child,
gazing beyond the horizon
overlooking a sea green ocean.
The Atlantic.

There water seemed to go on forever
yet it ceased at the point where
the blue sky kissed the horizon.
Occasionally, I would see a cruise ship
or a fishing trawler.
Maybe even a barge,
carrying it's cargo from one shore to another.

My mind full of questions about life.
My life.
I wondered what the future had
in store for me
I somehow felt overwhelmed
by those choices I'd be faced with
in the years to come.

Sometimes I thought about my
inevitable demise, and this scared the living shit out of me.
I was way too young to be
contemplating my own death.
And yet I did.

Eternity. No more. Never again.
I was terrified
And, when I'd be stuck in these thoughts, I'd was paralyzed.

It took every bit of my mental strength
to halt the drowning
in my pool of death.

My teachers told my parents,
"Shari is so smart.
She can do anything to which she aspires."
I carried these praises to this very day.

Consequently when I did not achieve my life's goal
(dream to become a veterinarian)
I lived in regret.
I have been lauded in my academic achievements
and my creativity yet,
regardless of what I have accomplished,
all too often,
I live in regret.

Shari Leigh   **Seasons & Crossroads Haiku**

1. Seasons
How I miss the fall
Winter comes early these days
Falling leaves so brief

2. Crossroads
Tempted toward a path
Which leads to a decision
Better left unmade

3. Seasons
Summer frolicking
Sandy beaches underfoot
Waves under my toes

4. Crossroads
I chose not the path
That was not my heart's desire
Leaves only regrets

5. Seasons
It's always winter
In here, I fear stif'ling
What is left of me

6. Crossroads
If a second chance
Came my way in this lifetime
I would cherish it

7. Seasons
Halloween, Christmas
Passover, Easter, the Fouth,
Memorial Day

8. Crossroads
Blooming in nature
Bursting yellow suns bright
Petals illuminate

Terra Leigh
Chesapeake, Va.

December

December marks
The beginning of an end,

And you want to end my success
With the thoughts

Of a knife
Kissing where no man will touch,
Wonders of what people might say,

Of a hut
On a snowy mountain top
Where I can sleep away
The stacked pain.

But a spotlight shines in my eyes,
The subject of strangers' attention,
The thrill reawakening
The beats of my passion.

My voice dances
With and without music,
The most talented in my system.

I can't abandon
This child I conceived
With God, my husband.

December marks
The beginning of an end,

The end to reckless abandon.

Terra Leigh

New Wine

He stomps all over me
With day jobs and student loans,

Pressing me against the boards
Until I burst.

But this is how
You make new wine,

And my liquids rest,
Fermenting and growing stronger
For God to taste
And pass to His people in communion.

He's not done with me yet.

Ed W. Lull
Williamsburg,
Va.

Ben and Agnes

Year 2012

At ninety-three and ninety-two
they stroll together hand-in-hand.
They will not let their age control
the active lives that they had planned.

His fertile mind led to design
of rockets in his early days,
then later took to trading stocks,
and made his wealth through market's maze.

He mows his lawn and trims his hedge
despite the heat of mid-July.
fall he blows his neighbor's leaves;
there's no hard work he wouldn't try.

He still attends a monthly lunch
of high school classmates who explore
things in life that helped them reach
that great plateau - The Final Four.

An undertaker, she was known
for gentle handling of deceased.
Her reputation served her well;
her business constantly increased.

But now she keeps a spotless home;
she cooks and cleans and tends her plants.
Then every Wednesday night they dress
and go downtown where they can dance.

They never followed aging rules,
but live their lives in their own way.
He spins his yarns of years gone by,
recalls them like they're yesterday.

They both outlived their first true loves,
but in each other found new dawn.
An inspiration to us all,
they took life's hardships, then moved on.

Year 2018

Five years ago Ben's true love died,
a tragedy for our dear friend.
The sadness took control of him;
his joyful life was at an end.

Ben grieved for Agnes many months
and blamed himself for her demise.
He'd made decisions for her care.
"Which way to go?" He'd agonize.

Ben thought his love was on the mend
but one dark night she slipped away.
Her doctor simply said: "She's gone;
she couldn't last another day."

Our friendship helped to ease his pain
but healing never was complete.
His luncheon buddies all were gone;
Ben never learned the word retreat.

He managed stocks and made his trades;
Ben walked and exercised each day.
His neighbors always smiled and waved;
respect and love we'd all display.

Easter 2018

The house next door is empty now,
Ben's ninety-seventh was his last.
To join his Agnes was his wish;
their leaving marks an era passed.

Christmas 2018

New lives now grace our neighborhood;
we welcome them this holiday.
Nostalgia reigns; we can't forget
old friends, too soon have passed away.

A Blessed Journey and Farewell

Ed Lull

A windy, wintry day in '53
we walked above the rocks on Severn's shore.
I knew commitment time was here - and we
agreed to share our lives forevermore.

On June the fourth of nineteen fifty-five
we said our solemn vows and thus began
a blessed journey on that joyful road
of love between a woman and a man.

The Navy kept us moving place-to-place,
and sometimes caused us lengthy times apart.
We learned the hurt of separation was
a test to the devotion of the heart.

Despite the painful loss of our first son,
our children came and claimed their share of love.
They soon became the focus of our lives;
they were most welcome gifts from God above.

In just one blink they all grew up and left
and each pursued the challenge of career.
But then in two quick blinks the grandkids came;
a whole new outlet for our love was here.

And then another generation came;
as six great-grandkids further blest our lives.
Our home became the place of great delight
when time for our Thanksgiving feast arrived.

Each anniversary we turn the page
as we have done for sixty-three great years.
However, this time everything would change;
the page is blank except for stain of tears.

On looking back we could be justly proud
that every single vow we took, we meant.
Commitment packed with love will never break;
I have no doubt that you were heaven-sent.

Ed Lull

To Face the Night
~A Villanelle~

I go, not willingly, to face the night.
Although the joys of living still are strong,
my limitations soon will dim the light.

My friends and loved ones, beacons shining bright,
but pain and illness render days too long.
I go, not willingly, to face the night.

I never shall complain about my plight;
life has been kind and little has gone wrong -
but limitations soon will dim the light.

No problems in my life I couldn't fight;
no place I've been where I did not belong.
I go, not willingly, to face the night.

If I've offended any, I'm contrite.
There are no grudges that I would prolong,
but limitations soon will dim the light.

My code has been: just do what I think right,
so sadness will not fill my evensong.
I go, not willingly, to face the night;
my limitations soon will dim the light.

Mirage to Oasis

*Crickyt J. Expression
Chesapeake, Va.*

Painting pretty mental pictures
of how it *could* be,
the truth was hard to see

Walking around with eyes wide shut,
I wanted to believe the fantasy,
stubbornly willing it to be

But, life doesn't come with magic pixie dust.

After one too many stumbles,
tortured eyes unveiled reality,
awakening
where I never wanted to be

Focusing crystal clear gaze
upon the unknown,
I turned
towards bettering me

Musing On How I've Changed

Crickyt J. Expression

Silver moonlight infused wisdom
into my cells,
permitting blessings found
through most difficult pain-
harsher than a lover's betrayal

Emotions flow
weaving differently
to create release
acceptance most prominent,
casting out anger;
ruler of the past

Emerging from quiet contemplation
into pity for the Other,
understanding their limitations
blooms forgiveness
for brash assumptions

Free of self-imposed responsibility
to correct their views,
I step lighter
into new growth,
tucking away leaflets of perspective
to share on my path

A Sestina for Mother Nature

Linda Partee
Williamsburg, Va.

   Your beauty has been praised as glorious
O Mother, nurturing Mother of ours:
winter's bleak fields draped in crystalline capes,
newborn buds nursing dew of moist mornings,
summer's sand-bathed shores ruffled by frothed waves,
ballet of autumn leaves in their striptease dance.

Such passion revered as you whirl and dance,
fine-tuning your music to glorious--
portraits of inspiration conveyed in waves.
O Mother, magnificent Mother of ours,
artist of twilight and morning,
your transfigurations wound tight in silk capes.

Your power snaps like a bullfighter's cape,
as brazen and bold as a hummingbird's dance.
Your fearless tides rise night and morn
untamed; we call your rolling swells glorious.
O Mother, demanding Mother of ours,
the awe for your sleight-of-hand seldom wavers.

Your fearsome behavior delivered in waves--
hissing like hot steam escaping shrew's cape.
O Mother, furious Mother of ours,
unleashing punishing whorls through your dance;
we struggle, defenseless within your glory,
to curse and blame…then beg another morning.

Praying your blessing of encore mornings,
your selfish offspring expect to ride smooth waves;
daring our minds to grasp then bask in your glory.
Never stagnant, you switch chameleon capes
to step out new and fresh in a debut dance;
O Mother, all-knowing Mother of ours.

O Mother, disappointed Mother of ours,
face of dawn and muse of mornings,
inviting us all to rejoin your dance
to save your grandeur and grain's amber waves.
Our greed robs and rapes in endless capers;
shamed we've transgressed your bounty and glory.

Teach us to dance again, dear Mother of ours,
To sing of your glory and bow to sweet morns.
Forgive us wavering love – bind our life-threads to your cape.

Linda Partee

A Spring Canvas
~A Sonnet~

A hangover of dullness floats away
on forest whispers, faint as silken thread;
once barren trees now wake pastel's cachet,
announcing promises about to spread.

A windowpane of spring will frame her art,
an iridescent web to spin a dream;
such palette spills the colors for the start
when pregnant blossoms birth this season's schemes.

Our world now cradles innocence still fresh,
as nature readies her parade's grand march
to ruffles, trills and flourishes which mesh
and pump the cold and dark from spirit's parch.

These skillful strokes by Mother Nature's hand
reward deep thirst and reverence for our land.

Linda Partee

Winter's Cusp
~A Sonnet~

The worst is coming, but so too, the best;
surrounded now by naked forest things
whose arms reach upward, praying to be blessed
by mercy's warmth that waits in off-stage wings.

Among the bare, we're bundled up and gloved;
the bored ones gnaw left-over holidays,
expired and chipped nostalgia mulled and loved--
our need-to-numb defense against malaise.

With spilled black ink, the night creates a shrine
where outburst stars on velvet sparkle down,
and streams of silent light pour chilled white wine,
exposing festooned beauty's snow globe crown.

Let lip and brick puffs of smoky breath blow;
words hurled at winter cannot stop the snow.

Linda Partee

The Young Bride

Her fairytale behind a veil of lace
to blind reality for just a while;
illusion spreads the glue to seal romance
with satin visions trailing tulle and silk.

A star ascends, illuminating aisle--
the bride's momentous role which spotlights change,
reminding guests that once-upon-a-time
they stood untested, wide-eyed, innocent.

To trip the aisle toward wedded life is bold,
a journey cushioned by tradition's rules--
all pomp and circumstance of rites unleashed,
propelling couples toward their "I do" pledge.

Through whispered oohhs and aahha the bride steps forth;
it's not about the gown, the veil or pearls;
it's not about bouquets nor tall-tiered cake.
It's heartstrings stretched from here to there and back--
it's pure romance. And later, love begins.

'Til Death Us Do Part

*Lucy Quinn
Williamsburg
Va.*

You kept pieces of the puzzle,
and walked gently in to the forest.
You left no breadcrumbs to follow,
did not want to find your way back,
did not want to be found.
Your note said you were sorry.

I didn't see you were coming apart,
so I wasn't looking for pieces.
After the world exploded
I found fragments in the rubble.
Friends, family caught in the blast staggered forward,
shell-shocked, handing me tattered puzzle scraps.

I tried to reassemble the image,
not that it would have made a difference.
The world was, and still would have shattered.
Why it happened, was in the missing pieces.

Constant motion builds walls to protect my soul.
Relentless lightning storms of mental activity are the mortar
that strengthens the fortress protecting the sanity inside.

Memories breach the idle mind and are driven back
by productive or self-destructive means.
Tequila and the blanket of sleep promise to
swaddle the silent screams.
Kicking and thrashing I break the embrace.

I sit again with the broken puzzle,
its ragged borders and spoiled image.
I flip it over, blank side up,

and pick and prune away pieces,
until a woeful canvas remains.

From a rainbow of pencils I select the first
one my hand touches, powder blue.
Aimlessly, it moves like a planchette over the vacant surface
leaving sky colored swirls behind.
More pencils, more colors.
A red lace pattern spreads across the tapestry like flame.

I pause before dropping the match,
scrutinize one last time the pieces of your life.
The puzzle glows and pulses as the edges curl,
the pieces collapse on themselves and dissolve.
My soul rises in the smoke,
released from a fortress no longer needed.

Robert Rickard
Burgess, Va.

At Home on Poros

*for Vasilis and Gianna Zagaraios,
in their seasons of wisdom,
knowledge, joy.*

After twenty hours in transit and several
days exploring Poros, travelers yield not
to sleep, afraid to miss a single igneous
gem beneath their feet in Greece. Aegina,
Hydra, Epidauros, Mycenae, Athens –
all are lights still beaconing to wanderers,
while Poros engulfs them like a home. Above,

Orion prowls the night – Artemis' favored
hunter on his autumn rise returns
to goad earthbound insomniacs who dot
the balconies of shores that ring one thousand
Aegean lands. Neither these islands nor
their issue outnumber those bodies that people the heavens,
whose nascent points of radiance await
their names on the tongues of men. What nature grants

to each moment swells the space of legends
for eons. "Metanoia" – change in the human
family as in its cosmos – mirrors
this culture's tortutred trek across five thousand
mortal years in permanent restoration.
After Persians, Romans, Turks, wherever
modern feet would stand, already Greece
waned and waxed again. On a peaceful Poros

inlet, morning approaches like a cherished
friend. Students of worlds tread time, ignore
the ticking of clocks, absorb each sign: cups
touching saucers, lips, saucers again;

cool breezes stirring bougainvillea accenting
porches of white marble; the sun, in pellucid
ministration, transforming terracotta
roofs astride the mountain rock outcroppings,
or blinking through clouds that shade vast cypress forests;
magpies darting straight as arrows from olive
trees to the sea, while off the mountain crest
fierce wings of eagles unfold to soar with Zeus
beyond Poseidon's reach. Just so, each day's
display awakes a guest's inchoate desires:
to know first-hand the rocky earth, blue sea,
fresh air as pure as Kalavria's mystic
pasts; to feast on bread, cheese, tomatoes,
olives, meat, when lunching at Taverenas
shaded beneath ubiquitous Plain trees;
to climb the daunting Clocktower rocks above
Sfenia's Saronic Gulf harbor to view the rooftops
of Poros Town; to meet Aegeans as gracious
as a Zagoraios who touches the hearts
of foreign guests with sumptuous repasts at home
and sends them thank-you notes for coming. At length

today's Odysseus hears the Sirens' songs
of rapt connections, the *Chronos* of daily steps
through worlds in search of new and sweet adventures,
perhaps not breaking free again. But Poros,
like its ancient gods and citizens,
is jealous for its due, its pull in time,,
its *Kairos* of ageless significance. In lighting
the lanterns of home for all – like Hermes
speeding the words of gods – Poros wakes affable
witnesses, extending its shores across
the globe in haunting immortality.

The Poet's Domain

Robert Rickard

The Certain Spring

"Earth cares for her own ruins, naught for ours.
Nothing is certain, only the certain spring
--Lawrence Binyon

I.
A camera chooses familiar paths across
a cherished bayside sliver of eastern Virginia.
Click, Click the SONY forms it's Treasures

for hundreds of pictures of this day's angles in sun
and shade. It seems earth shouts an inclination
toward life . . . emergent, radiant, surprising.

This orb – blue dot on which mankind depends,
a sibling among billions in an infinite family –
is parent to brilliant splashes of springtime color.

Dozens of well-dressed trees were on stage this spring.
Star Magnolia and Bradford Pear dismissed winter.
Plum, Peach and Apple promised generous harvests.

Redbud and Kwanza Cherry blushed for weeks.
Maple, Oak and Sycamore, commanding airspace,
waved new leaves to young crops of wheat and corn.

Were these grounds a fish bowl in nature's theater,
an audience might spot a modern Job in a sea
of blossoms swallowed into the belly of beauty.

II.
Raise high the scrim on a longer, sadder play –
a story about earth as acting and acted upon,
in scenes of spring coming, but always slipping away.

Springtime is mocked by capricious nature, interminably.
Storms of all strengths can steal the breath of innocents.
Cancers can sleep in bodies but wake-up malignant

All earth's species are risked in their sun's destiny.
And, man has ***his*** fingers in warfare, oil-spills, global
warming, terrorism, poverty, corporate greed.

In this script about mutable nature and mutable man,
seeming the implacable potentate, giving and taking,
earth only reveres ***its*** purposes and laws.

III.

How great an irony that earth – like Spinoza's god
who loves and hates no one – may not care,
but produces animate beings whose care is incessant.

One likes to believe that De Vinci's Mona Lisa,
Bach's "St. Matthew Passion," Eliot's "Ash Wednesday,"
and Jefferson's "Declaration of Independence"

will survive to enrich the spirit of future generations.
As if the white-hot Spirea in a country garden
were a permanent beacon of life to the heavens.

Rejoice when the one-year glass is but one season filled.
With earth on stage playing good dwarf and bad dwarf,
Few scenes are more poignant than "the certain spring."

Robert Rickard

My Library
. . . speaking to my books, and
remembering Jane McFarland

Soon you'll have to go
as I grow far in years.
From youth to maturity
I saw your pilgrimage.

You know history of writing --
cuneiform tablets in Sumer,
to Egyptian hieroglyphics,
swimming toward Wittenberg's Theses.

Along that ancient path
especially **you** would have noticed
that steady, widespread run
among your exceptional forbears.

From every antecedent
to these well-loved shelves,
your kin shaped willing minds
across this earthly orb.

Here most of you were loved
-- no time or mind for all.
From beginnings until now,
boundaries were probed.

Your presence screams reminders
to care, to search, to find.
Will future folk ever study
a Homer, or Virgil, or Dante?

Who in these busy days
will pause, will disconnect
computers, cell phones, TVs
to hear unknown muses again?

Even on your highest shelf
I stare at a stack of Writings.
Those schoolboy scribbles of mine
will reach no new readers again.

From the start of my younger studies
a few books became this Collection.
But Libraries blanket the earth --
0n- line, digitized!

Will you, old friends, get moved
into new owner kindness,
or reach some final destruction --
your fate as uncertain as mine?

Robert Rickard

The Sacrifice
*...remembering countless Roman Catholic
and other Boys and Girls*

Erect, before one chosen
    for a private rite,
        he latched the chapel door
against the public light.

The lad beside the cloth
    leaned free of facts or fear,
        until the altar strongman
pulled him down, then near.

The chosen had no choice,
    all absences consenting;
        the moment came too soon,
abrupt and unrelenting.

Fathers, teachers, rulers –
    miasmic authorities –
        whose craft can reach a child
adrift on chartless seas?

Voices from Rome dissemble
    (except of the fetus and war),
        while heaven's scrim has lifted
from stages lit no more.

Where to go as whom?
    that's a child's tough question,
        willing himself or disposed
toward gifts of new creation.

The hand that spins the stars
        is fierce, might yet seem kind:
       shaping abundant chaos
With an art of recondite mind.

Dawn Riddle
Smithfield, Va.

Etchings

Lines like veins on leaves
cover weathered faces with texture –
aging skin's artwork

Dawn Riddle

Until

Everyday routine often
seems like days are déjà vu,
slogging through quicksand:
scores of repetitive chores,
weight of responsibilities...

...**until overturned.**
Interruption by the unexpected –
necessitates
sudden shifts in priorities,
navigating after shocks,
regaining agile footing.

... **until surpassed.**
Calendar pages flip,
momentum of youth slows,
nature's imposed repose
retires treadmills of yesterday.

Kailyn Sasso
Virginia Beach, Va.

Inverno

Silence enfolds you
with falling snow;
        sparkles in your hair
        frostbite on your nose.
There are so many ways
to indulge the winter
        but can we
        ever truly grasp its beauty?
The sky is gray and dull.
The air is cold and null.
        Breathe it in
        and never let it go.
Icicles drape the
windows,
        glistening in
        rays of light.
Snow is the
siren of the seasons.
        How can something
        be so beautiful
        yet so dangerous?
I do not know which to prefer,
the sparkling snow
        or watching
        the leaves come and go.
Autumn leaves,
dying leaves,
        the snow takes
        them all.

My body goes numb
as the snow
catches my fall.
    If I am buried
    by this winter
I will make it my bed,
    and wait for Spring
    to wake my sleepy head.

Kailyn Sasso

Wilted

plant the seed
in the mud
of your eye
roses of love
come here to die
they wilt
then f
       a
          l
             l
nothing will grow
nothing at all

Ann
Shalaski
Newport
News, Va.

Departure

The reason I'm writing this on the back
of a train schedule now that you've left
for good, is to tell you the small table
by the kitchen window where we ate breakfast
every morning, radio tuned to weather, turned
to me and said, "What do you want to do now?"

The oak trees seemed to be listening.
Sky became clear and still as they pressed forward
expecting a reply, and I thought of me watching
you walk out the front door into rose-yellow sun
on your way to bigger plans. Knowing I had
all the time in the world to answer.

Ann Shalaski

Just So You Know

I believe in before, tomorrow,
and second chances.

In dandelion wishes, redemption,
life in a faraway galaxy.

That names have power,
everything makes sense,

and mothers mark children
when they enter into the world.

I believe the bottom line is at the bottom.
That honesty is not tender,

and the pain of grief is ours
and ours alone.

I think it's odd how people peg us
by what we believe.

When not one of us can see what the other
sees, or looks beyond that space in between.

Ann Shalaski

Pedal Past Perfect

We kids rode bikes on city streets
half-lit with fading summer sun.
Smell of supper on our clothes,

we raced over railroad tracks,
circled Lou's Market at the end
of the block.

A ten-year old can pedal a thousand miles
beyond the curve of the Earth,
or so I thought.

Slightest tilt left or right of my blue
American Flyer thrust me into the skyline.
Where north became south,

south became north. Dividing line between
present and future clearly in front of me.
I'd fly through intersections in a blur

of spinning wheel spokes. Bell blaring
on my handlebar. Eager to pass pigtails,
neighborhood boundaries,

life a little at a time, I wanted to reach
the center of everything. Speed by
our front porch steps,

leave picture perfect behind.
What matters most now, is that I can recall
with detail, fragrant flowers that bloom

year after year by the walk. My mother's voice
calling me back. And the moon following me
home.

A Simple Song

Ann Shalaski

I want to write a love poem
to all the boys in my homeroom
for what we didn't do but wished

we could. For Sister Mary Margaret
and the sins of intention she said
would send us to hell.

I'll write a hymn to deep, dark secrets
in blue ink on white paper,
read aloud in late afternoons

when I was a girl, flimsy as a kite.
I'll pen a tribute to sixteenth birthday
parties in dark-paneled basements,

where we played spin-the-bottle
and post office, next to the Sears
washer and dryer.

I want to write a simple song,
one that speaks to the opening
and closing of back porch doors

and roads that go somewhere.
I'll write a refrain about how to leave
without looking back.

The Autumn of Our Lives

Barbara Drucker Smith
Newport News, Va.

The dead leaves of autumn
Lead to renewal in spring
The death of a person can lead
To renewal in another lifetime
Such as how and where did Mozart
Hone his talent in his lifetime
Perhaps from a past life of his
My conviction of after life
Came after a near death experience
I was in a tunnel and then came out
To experience God and indescribable peace
When the lifeguards were resuscitating me
I could see them from the ceiling
When I ended up back in my body
I was fist fighting the lifeguards
Which is against my nature

Karen Sparrow
Hampton, Va.

Old Black Train

You don't need no luggage
Just leave it where it's at
There's no use for it
At the end of the tracks

If you hear that
Old whistle blowing on down the line
Calling you to board it
Just turn and floor it
Cause
There ain't no turning back

That old black train
Just whizzing down the tracks
Picking up passengers
On its way clickety clack
Once you reach the end
There ain't no turning back

There ain't no turning back

Karen Sparrow

Saying Hello

I'm running
I'm jumping
I'm the snowflake on
Your tongue
I'm whooshing down hills
I'm gliding across ice
I'm balls of snow
Whacking your chest
I'm frost bitten noses
And very cold toes
I'm snowmen with scarves
I'm hot chocolate
And marshmallows
I'm rosy cheeks
I'm a warm dinner
I'm saying hello
To winter

Karen Sparrow

The Seasons Cycle

Autumn

Leaves
Turn brown
Fall to ground

Wind
Blows cold
Chills to bone

Frost
on ground
Feet so cold

End
So near
Can be seen

Sleep
Comes soon
Rest is here

Dawn
Has come
Sky so bright

Day
Crisp clean
New and fresh

Birds
Fly high
Sing so sweet

New
Day begins
Time starts anew

Spring

Spring
Is in
The morning air

The
Earth began
To thaw out

Flowers
Plants trees
All grow anew

Bees
Make golden
Delicious sticky honey

Watch
Your step
Snakes are out

Birds
Are singing
Beautiful morning songs

Days
Getting longer
By the minute

Colors
So bright
Fresh and new

Time
For earth
To start anew

Summer

June
Is hot
Sunny fun outdoors

Summer
Is here
Will get hotter

July
Is hotter
I'm wearing shorts

Humidity
Increasing I'm
Melting away fast

August
Is sweaty
Fiery and sweltering

Summer
Is great
Wear less clothes

Judith Stevens
Norfolk, Va.

Avian Christianity at the Crossroads

A large group
of Canadian geese
gathered at
The Jehovah Witness Kingdom Hall
in Norfolk,
where the congregation stood silently,
counting the numbers of their flock.

Only one hundred forty-four
could continue their journey.

The rest were consigned to stay there
by the Elizabeth River.

Alas,
they were not part
of the redeemed

Remembered Taste of Blackberries

Judith Stevens

      January cold creeps in at windows
numbing Summer's toes, Winter's woes.
      Icy wind rattles sunlit panes,
tosses leftover leaves that escaped the rake.

Unbidden, I remember Summer's
          juicy fat blackberries,
     holding their warm secrets
          in tiny balled fists –
nestled in Southern patches of my childhood.

They glowed purplish-black
          against pink palms!
     When we bit into one,
 juice squirted from our mouths –
        staining our shirts and fingers.

We prob'ly ate two for ev'ry one we picked an' pocketed.
      As the sun rose higher, we sweated through
          thin cotton shirts.
     The "pong" in the bottom of our pails
turned to soft "plops" as our buckets filled.

      Flies and bumblebees droned on;
          cicadas chanted, "Home,home,"
'til we took the hint and left, careful to back our way out,
          past the thorns ready to snag.

Grandmother waited, smiling.
Her fragrant dough embracing our berries,
    folding them in, baking to a golden sizzle.
That night the family ate steaming blackberry cobbler,

We felt as proud as if we'd made it ourselves!

Ken Sutton
Machipongo, Va.

Black River

When the Black River wanders past Dexter
does it notice the young boy flailing the water
without mercy or success below the fall,

dragging a Royal Coachman through the roil
lightly silted by rain soaked pasture land
in his futile quest for steelhead rainbow?

The wrong fly, perfectly tied with hope
fortified by ignorance, cast in confidence
as yet unmarred by experience.

No trout will see his feathered hook,
a number 16, perfect for still pools
between riffles of a wooded creek.

Here, in the April river rush when foam explodes
over buried boulders, lost in the flashing flotsam
of winter last grip, the coachman drowns to no end.

The river is constant, its water fleeting,
a swift rush of time unencumbered
by memory of yesterday or fear of tomorrow.

And, though he casts feathered hope upon the water,
is the boy never more than rain upon the river's back
while it rushes in place, forever seeking the sea?

Ken Sutton

Coffee in the DMZ

As the old man reaches into the fridge
to get milk for his son's coffee,
the long checkmark scar on his forearm,

time-blurred against last summer's tan,
    slides across his field of vision,
        turns his world jade,
            rotting vegetation
                scents the air.

Two percent, Dad.

        It could almost be Louisiana
        except the bamboo's not right
        and there's no elephant grass
        back in Opelousas.

Y'hear me, Dad?

        The dirt is damp.
        Dark as the bank
        of Bayou Tortue.

The old man grabs the milk,
sets it in front of his son,
sits and sips coffee, black

        as the hard beaten path
        stretched out before his squad
        dividing their green world
        into left and right.

Paul Boudreaux passed.
His boy, Armand,

>He owns the left,
>Martinez the right.
>Danny Rosenthal's got point.

come by to pick him up.
Found him at the kitchen table.

>He worries about Danny,
>young, two weeks in country
>and still eager for contact.

Dressed for church,
coffee all down his front,

Behind him the refrigerator door
swings slowly and snicks shut,

>echoing the almost silent
>parting of the trip wire.
>Bouncing Betty bursts forth

cup on the floor.
Cold as Papa Mal.

>exploding, as designed, one meter above ground.
>Taking, as designed, Danny's guts
>and flinging them, shredded red tinsel

Nothing for it but call the funeral home.
Mouton Brothers. They came quick.

        dripping from bamboo, crooked in the growing.
        Driving, as an afterthought, a jagged steel shard
        trailing intestine through the hole in Danny's back.

Armand told me 'bout it after midnight mass
when we were coming out, face white as rice.

        Flashes through the air
        like an angry cottonmouth,
        scorches then sizzles flesh,

Hell of a thing. Old man
sitting in his house all day,

        gouges him wrist to elbow
        leaving a bright red furrow
        that heals into a leper's scar

cold as wet clay,
waiting for church.

        for him to stare at
        in fifty years time
        getting milk
        for his son's coffee

        when he stops by
        Christmas morning
        to scold his father
        for missing mass.

Ken Sutton

Maps & Photographs

I think it unhealthy to live alone with maps
decorating his walls like family photographs.
Tourist maps in Swedish of Helsinki and Tallin.

"Isn't Helsinki in Finland?"

>"Yes. Sixty degrees north.
>Accent on the first syllable."

Saigon, curled at the edges,
yellow with age and coffee,
street names penciled in French.

Also Notting Hill, cut from
a larger plat of London
with pinking shears.

"Why Notting Hill and pinking shears?"

>"The map was too large
>and they were at hand."

There is a reticence about him
that closes the door on further inquiry.

He drinks coffee
and keeps milk.

If you want sugar
you must bring your own,
though he does have honey.

His house is but one large room,
singleton bed tucked behind bookcases,
cubby kitchen, maple table by the door
with two oak chairs that almost match.

Africa, three feet wide, five tall,
hangs on the inside of his door.

"Why Africa?"

    "I don't know where
     things are over there."

Africa is free of pencil and ink.
His city maps are pocked with glyphs,
looped crosses, arabesque x's.

"What do they mark?"

    "Beginnings and endings."

He's a master of answers that don't.

He owns no computer, nor even a television.
There is a rotary phone on his table,
black and heavy with silence.

He listens attentively to foreign broadcasts
brought him by a large mahogany radio
with glowing tubes and a multitude of dials.

"What language is that?"

"My parents' native tongue."

He speaks without discernible accent
of the day they paved his once two track road,
of the new houses built after the war.

"Which war?"

"The one that changed things."

Though we live on the same road,
I have many neighbors, he but one.

On moonless nights
his glowing curtain
softens my yard.

And because I think it unhealthy
to be left alone with maps for company
I visit him and ask my questions,

watch his answers slide away
into dark corners of the room

while I drink coffee,
black, without sugar,
sometimes with honey.

Ken Sutton

Sgt. Mitchell's Visit

Ohio Veterans Home
3416 Columbus Ave
Sandusky, OH 44870
2017

I'm the Sergeant Major of this outfit.
Still got my command voice.
Make people round here jump,
if I've a mind to.

When I was younger and taller
I had medals,
and a chest to pin 'em on.

I slept without dreaming of faces,
calling out names,
woke only if somebody slapped my feet
and yelled, **Incoming!**

Nobody yells here.
I've got my own room.
No one hears me call roll.
Knows I count the dead.

    *

My nephew visited me twice,
birthdays, five years apart.
Took me to the *Mon Ami*.
Had steak and potato
with a bucket of sour cream
and a bottle of wine,
good wine, some French name.

Second Saturday in October

they pack us up to Cedar Point.
The park folks slap a wrist band
on you and everything's free.
Rides. Food. The works.
No beer though.

Every year I figgered I'll take a shot
at that big coaster, The Maverick.
Every year I'd let 'em talk me out of it.

But not no more.
Last year I had a stroke
on the Ferris wheel.

Couldn't go this year
unless I sat in a wheel chair,
let some keeper push me around.
I stayed back.

Keep trying to give me a walker.
I'll die if I take it. Be dead in a week.
Till then I'll corkscrew around on my cane.

Last summer, when it got hot,
late July, first half of August,
I'd rehabbed enough
to get back on the yard.

Little pond out there with a sidewalk.
Quarter mile makes a round trip.
If I start early,
I can lap it twice before lunch.

       *

I'm the Sergeant Major here.
Still got my command voice.

My medals are in the room,
if you want to look at 'em.
Keep 'em in a drawer,
bedside, next to my Gideon.

Get 'em out sometimes
at night when I wake up,
namin' names, remembering
places that never mattered.

      *

You…?

You look familiar.

Do I know you?

Bells Ring

Tammy Tillotson Chase City, Va.

Cloche, names a bell—
Of me it were said,
The loveliest cloche
Was but wrung on my head.

In ebony old
With its feathery tufts,
Its box and its pills
Were mere pleasantries in such.

For the cloche was admired
As I walked 'long the street.
I sat on a wall,
Never a stranger to meet.

Yet as I sat in my seat
That December
It seems, I somehow had
Lost the true trueness of me.

For while November had struggles
Those long winter months too
The tune in my ears
Cried to walk in your shoes.

For then by the spring
The sun found again
The places I wandered,
Forgot, where I'd been.

The Poet's Domain

>Today, a worn cloche
>May still rest on my head.
>For as long as I breathe,
>It will mean I'm not dead.

Tammy Tillotson

Cost of Living

I was sitting at home, turned on the 6 o'clock news,
To hear round-about the time, I might
Expect the hurricane coming thru.

When a dog-tired anchor, with matted hair
Sopping wet, questioned a stranger,
Whose words I can't soon forget.

I've been thru Michael and Sandy,
Floyd, Florence and Fran
But this here is home
Yes, ma'am, I love where I am.

I've seen one season come,
I'll watch another one go.
It's just the cost of living here in Paradise.

With the wind whipping round, debris swirling by,
The anchor asked once more for comment
On the weather going on outside.

No ma'am, I'm not happy. No ma'am, I'm not
Really sad. By now, a storm's just a storm.
Which is why I'll pray it ain't bad.

I've been thru Michael and Sandy
Floyd, Florence and Fran.
Yes, this here is home
And I love where I am.

I've seen one season come,
I'll watch another one go.
It's just the cost of living here in Paradise.

For even weather has high tides,
It can't always weather in lows,
Still, surely, hurricanes come,
Then just as fast they will go.

So, whether starting at A, or ending
Pretty-Darn-Quick, I'm only tired of feeling
Tired, and tired of it making me feel sick.

Yes, a storm's just a storm.
It won't be so bad, A might yet.
I've survived backward and forward
Yes, I've seen the whole alphabet

So tonight, as it's dark, with heavy eyelids
I'll sleep. My prayers said for the morning
I'll not have more reasons to weep.

No, we don't get to pick and no, we don't
Get to choose. Life's challenges are just
the cost of living here in Paradise.

Travelers

Tammy Tillotson

Oh, to be a bridge!
Oh, to be a train!
To brave the highest mountain ridge,
To see inside each window pane.

To know the grass and want its green,
Right, exactly where you are,
Makes short a weary traveler's dreams
When the miles and miles seem far.

Still, who can sleep?
Clam, clamp, clambering track,
Carrying friendships, it keeps
Fond memories calling us back.

Guard each crossing.
Light the way.
Though we may feel lost,
We always know we're safe.

Oh, to be a bridge!
Oh, to be a train!
Yes, what a privilege it is
To be aboard as evening wanes.

Another Letter to God

12 Keys
Portsmouth, Va.

Dear God-

I used to refer to You as Daddy until I found out I had one
Now I just reference You like yo, Son because I'm done
Your jealous rage
Has turned my holidays
Into hallow ways
In my soul
This death rampage that You're on is getting old
And I'm taking it personal
In Your word, You say Your love is unconditional
But it seems unpredictable
And provisional
I look to You for roots and You give me leaves
I turn to You for comfort and You give me grief
I can't with You
I do what I'm supposed to do
And You pluck flowers from my garden like
      I don't already know they belong to You
STOP IT!
If I turn my back on You, I'm destined for damnation
But my frustration
Is definitely turning me in that direction
Even though the good saints say look to You for protection
What a misconception!
I mean, that's like watching a hitman kill my significant other
Then purposely seeking him out for cover
Preposterous…right?

Now, it's the wrong season for planting seeds
And You already know that I be constantly plucking weeds
'Cause nonsense and negativity are two things I don't need

So, slow Your roll in picking the fruits of my labor
Please allow my love to simmer so I can savor the flavor
For a bit until You decide to snatch or weed me out
If it sounds like I have seeds of doubt,
I do
And You should know that they were implemented by You
But I really don't have anyone else to turn to
So, at the end of the day, I guess I'll continue to talk to You,

Son!

I Am Not Broken

12 Keys

I refuse to wear the title broken
Even though, they say, "if the shoe fits…"
And my soul so easily pours into it
But my mind won't acknowledge or grasp that shit
Because to me
Broken means loose parts or not working
And personally, I've never stopped
I was never given that op – tion
To do so
So on and on I go
Mending the bruises
Caring for the contusions
Some even get ice packs
And I can't begin to count the number of knives
      I've had to pull out of my back
I've got surgical scars from heartache
Seen stars from nose breaks
Been arrested to survive
Pulled a trigger to stay alive
But I'm not broken
I may not run like I used to
Or even walk as fast I used to
I can't dance like I used to
Or stand for very long like I used to
But I press on from day to day
Sometimes I feel out of sorts and can't find my way
But I keep going with perseverance
Now, I may be a whole lot bent
But I am not broken

12 Keys

Seasonal Change

My whole life has been rearranged
You always taught me to grow with change
You taught me to accept blessings that come my way
Live life better and better each day
You were my Springtime
My moonbeam-my sunshine
Yes, our relationship had its heated Summers
                              from time to time
But when you departed, my life slipped into a Fall
My heart grows cold as I hear Winter call
But you taught me that everything has its season I
just have to find that reason
To bounce back!

Jack Underhill
Falls Church, Va.

Cold Morning Unfolding

I watched the cold morning unfold

It was 7:00 AM and 22 degrees outside.
The sun was bravely trying to break through the trees.
The Rhododendrons were huddling and
Shriveled up unto themselves.
The Sun reflected in the
Cut glass in the door.

It was 8:00 AM and 32 degrees outside.
The sun had climbed above the trees
And was warming forth.
The Rhododendrons had faith
And were opening up their leaves.

It was 9:00 AM and 40 degrees outside
The sun was more of itself
More like burning desire
And warm love on Valentine's Day.
The Rhododendrons opened up even more
But still with leaves pointed earthward
Like a bird's wings on the down swing

It was 9:30 AM and a small fluffy bird
Was perched disconsolately on the feeder
Empty of seed.
I refilled the feeder.
Soon, six twittering enthusiasts were competing
For space on the squirrel-proof perch.

It was 10:00 AM and the morning sun
Cast blue shadows on the
White ready-to-melt snow
And off in the distance a
Blood red cardinal was a dot of color on the landscape.
The snow clung to the top
Of the shed and the grandchildren's tree house.

I was brave and ready to run
Having emptied myself of the poem.

Embraced by Fall's First Blush of Cold:
A tribute to honor the Beliefs of the First Americans

Jack Underhill

I stepped out expecting summer's heat
But was surprised by
The embrace of fall's
First blush of cold.

I stopped to drink in
The cool air refreshing my lungs.
The morning sun slanted
Through the trees
Highlighting the Japanese maple
In a mix of delicate brown and red.

The dogwood and oak
Had not yet turned to fall colors
But dripped in sunlight.
Above and among the highest oak
The squirrels jumped without
Fear from branch to branch
As if to repeal gravity's laws.

Even in the suburbs
I felt nature's throbbing pulse
And was reminded of
My at-oneness with the earth with the
The place-grounded religion
Of the First Americans who
Are being honored this week.
I offer tribute by quoting from a Litany of Faith

Inspired by Chief Seattle who said that:
> "Every shining pine needle every sandy shore
> Every mist in the dark woods,
> Every clearing and humming insect is holy.
> Whatever befalls the earth befalls the
> Children of the earth,
> And the earth is part of us.
> We belong to the earth.
> Like the blood, which unites one family,
> All things are connected.
> For we did not weave the web of life
> We are merely a strand in it."

Jack Underhill **Floating Feathers in Late Spring**

The blossoms of the weeping cherry
Float in the air like feathers
Caught between two not-yet-bloomed crepe myrtles

The Bradford pear stands grand and white
Proud over the porch.
Billowing white blossoms
Light up the street.

The yellow, purple and lavender tulips
Lift their blossoms above the their greening nests
Having survived the ever-hungry fleet of deer
And the creatures that crawl in the night in the autumn.

Hundreds of daffodils
Hang their heavy heads and
Grace the yard
With their chemical weapons
That repel the deer and squirrels.

An old tired dogwood struggles with only a few years left
With its remaining buds about to burst
But is overshadowed by a volunteer
Dogwood from beneath the edge of the porch.
The late-blooming red dogwood has yet to bloom.

The azaleas, crepe myrtle, roses and rhododendrons
Keep their bloom on hold
Biding their time.

In the garden of Eden
We complain about the dogs and potholes.

Charles Wilson
Virginia Beach, Va.

'56 Pickup

She drives a '56 Ford pickup,
dried mud, red primer,
Camels crumpled on the dash.

She's got traction, boot on the clutch,
glove on the wheel, 292, and
the chrome bird on the hood knows the way.

Goodbye road-side stand, fireworks and peaches.
Goodbye red-booth diner, bad tips and coffee cups.
She left her man corked in a bottle like a dead fish.

Her antenna cuts the belly of the Carolina sky.
She's got a roadmap on the shotgun side,
sunrise split by the cracked rear-view.

Charles Wilson

Family Plot

The sky's the belly of a rainbow trout,
slit and streaked with red and black.
I kneel by the river, scoop stars with a net,
tie tinsel-flies to a shimmering hook.

An oil-lamp glows in the farmhouse,
sickroom frowns upon the night.
A crow leers from a wooden post,
river grabs the red horns of a sickle moon.

I await the rider's boots and jangle,
his stethoscope, syringe, leather bag.
I've already painted the wagon black,
dusted with roses for the journey.

Charles Wilson

How to Be an Artist

Sketch an oval on paper,
sketch an oval on slate,
one eye for a bird,
one eye for a face.

Draw a girl with a mouth
who forgot how to smile.
Draw a boy with a heart
that he wears in his boot.

Paint a train at the station
pulling out of Mars Hill,
her face pressed on glass,
the rain rolling down.

Carve a heart in dead pine
with a dull pocket blade,
make an arrow that bursts
every soap bubble wish.

Scratch a stickman in chalk
who's late with bouquets
for the girl who's already
been feathered away.

Jukebox

Charles Wilson

Punched in "Old Love Letters"
by the Stanley Brothers,
clinked a Roanoke spoon,

became the nexus
of two worlds, two wings,
pulling in opposite directions.

But the coffee was strong

and the diesels poured in
and the singer burned letters,
gently, one by one.

I unfolded a five spot for Irene,
pushed open the handprint door
and became a bird in the gritty wind.

Charles Wilson

People are Different at Saying Goodbye

Some slip through mail slots,
others climb on trains,
some shatter crockery
or join the circus.

Some spill secrets,
others apologize,
some ride Greyhounds
or follow the band.

Lovers aren't buses
arriving on schedule.
Wrens and moons come and go -
the birdbath is full of rain.

J. Scott Wilson
Yorktown, Va.

Aderezo

I hope my season lasts its full run of days
So I can be sure to stick
      to the tip
      of your tongue
Before my time has run
So maybe when the weather changes again
you'll realize
how badly
you need another taste.

See a love affair that lasts only for a season
Is like having a taste for a particular season
and after you had it once then for no obvious reason
You repeat that dish for awhile
      reminisce about it and smile
      repeat trips to the same restaurant
      becomes a favorite haunt
Until the calendar flips its page
      your heart finds a new flavor to crave

So you cooled me
      when writing tales in a field so hot became unbearable
And you dried me off
      when monsoon soaked rags became unwearable
Shows how little I knew
      you just blew through
While comforted to meet your spice
      variety of life, it was nice
But perpetual change marks the passings of your life.

See a love affair that lasts only a season
        ends for me without obvious reason
I can't know from here when my flavor
        that made your tongue ting
        captivated you and made you savor
        turns out to not be a thing

        anymore

Then someone notices you no longer cook that way
        no longer order that dish
Just then you look up and you realize
        that you don't know why
But then you know that it's been time to fly

I just hope my season has a full run of days
        at least ninety-one
So I can be sure to stick there
        tip of your tongue
So maybe before the weather changes yet again
        you'll realize I'm the taste you want to remain

Eleven Hours on the Ferry

J. Scott Wilson

Oh say can you see
by the lights in my eyes?

Look across the water
See blue or slate-gray

Look down at the water
passing beneath your ferry's long legs
Long legs are made for running,
we keep turning around to ride over.

In places mocha like your nasty coffee
Alternately my refreshment; Coke-bottle green

Sunset-fire days we take this ride
turning around to ride over and over
Oh-God-thirty ferry is a lone star in the black river of void-
space
River divides moments of decision.
The East, West banks, the sky and reflective depth
become distant galaxies
become brackets that holds off sentences, decisions,
not seeing each other on the dark, dark decks.
You can see by the lights in my eyes
to read hearts; mine, yours.

You fire-moth, know draw of danger.
We pretend to commute five-days worth
turning around to ride over
Night's summer-short
and sun passes from misanthrope to prominent
Prominent enough that you decide
you don't need the lights in my eyes anymore.

I see, and that's your decision?

Now you can contemplate the changeable colors of my eyes,
but you'd rather study the changing colors of the water,
rather wave at the distant strangers
on the reverse-trip-ship,
a galaxy away from our discussion, your decision,
rather than turn and flash me one last smile.

Ferry at the docks
Our 'ship on the rocks
Your five minutes to debark spent turning the car,
One more, time as if pursuing the other ferry.
No, you use neutral-zone of transit to be nowhere.
Where we can be outside of time

You find me on top-deck
and fix the lights of my eyes with the sight of your eyes
Mine, the colors of waters turning green to brown
Yours, waters that turn green to blue
Our eyes are like the waters
May as well be one with the water
Time frozen on the water

Eyes
Water

First Day of Winter

J. Scott Wilson

Times for changes have come and gone
The sun has set on Fall's colorful days
This cold time is now to stay
To an end fixed in your ways

I hope you found a tolerable self
Or prepare to live with affection nevermore
They move you out and shut the door
Rage against that night became a chore

World moves and moves and leaves you there
Kids or grandkids put you in a place
Wind had changed and affixed your face
Can you take a thirty year slide with grace?

This is the first day of winter,
It could be a long one
Hunker down to ride it out
But don't count on next spring

J. Scott Wilson

Hydroplane

Sideways

Sheet of ice was not in the plan
Just one puddle too many
      two degrees too few
      three hours of unattended roadway
      four seconds of terrifyingly smooth sailing
      or less
Sideways

Best you can do is buckled up

Like a roller coaster you didn't wait in line for
Was your life, your choices, leading to this moment?
Spinning out of control, out of control
Or did you think you had a better grasp on your soul?
What are you thinking about that now for?
Well you don't have anything else to do
while your life flashes before your eyes
as the world paints itself across your windshield
      like the movie you missed
           while watching the movie
                you thought you were
                      meant to see.

This slide might as well be your life now
      or the new start.
Are we here to see what made you lose control?
Are we here to see the slide?
Are we here to see the crash?
Are we here to review your life before?
Are we here to see the aftermath?

Too late, the transition time is only that
See where the ride settles in the end,
    see what of your things are left
        scattered about the wreckage,
    pick them up,
        or leave them and walk on like day one.

Are you new?
    Renewed?
Are you recycled or like never?
Will there be lessons that last forever?
Or will we see you on the powerslide
    at the end of the next ride?
Will you respond, recoil from the winter chill
    or are these few seconds your addictive thrill?

J. Scott Wilson — Real Ironic Hobby: Trainwatching

When you saw me,
        my guitar,
        my bag,
        and my dog at the train station,
even on the platform
It was an uphill battle to convince you
        that I was not gone, baby
        that this was just a soulful moment
of just watching for trains to go by

It was an uphill battle talking my way
        back
        into your bed
        stay in your head
since I needed a place to stay
        one more day
        to get to next morning
'cause I need one more try, baby.

See, I'm always late,
        and the trains run on time.

Winter Season

Henriann Woleben
Suffolk, Va.

I enter the Memory Unit
where dementia reigns as Regal Thief,
robbing my mother and other residents
of precious memories.

It is 90 degrees outside
and a sweltering 88 degrees in my mother's room;
she is seated in her recliner,
wrapped in a heavy blanket.

She looks up with a blank stare,
her mind barren of any memory of me;
I cross the room
and take her hands in mine.

These delicate, smooth, manicured hands
that once held mine
and gave me a sense of security
are the strongest memory of my mother.

I search her face for any sign of
remembering me,
but darkness
has settled in for the long night.

The repetition begins as
she calls out for her mother;
I feel her loss and insecurity
as I, too, call out for mine.

My mother
is in her winter season.

Seasons Have Their Reasons

Gus Woodward II
Virginia Beach, Va.

Treating each season
  as if it came for a brand new reason.
Using unpredictable change
as chance to help rearrange. these crossed wires.
Gotta stop spinning tires,
get rid of all the liars,
while stoking the internal fires.
Now like the fall I let my leaves shed,
and by leaves I mean all the stuff
that doesn't belong inside my heart and head.
Winter has never been dead,
It just wants to be left alone for a while,
while using the solitude to reconcile.
At some point spring will come around,
never fails to astound,
turning the earth into a beautiful playground.
Summer comes but don't meltdown,
turn the music up and dig in now.
Absorb as much energy as life will allow.
We all have our own field to plough,
constant improvement is my vow.
To myself along this lane,
as more self love I gain,
crossroads always contain,
a choice but I have become a train
with no need for tracks or pathways.
I am here to trail blaze!
Giving constant praise,
as I am blessed to raise,
a son that shines so bright
he sets my world ablaze.

Beyond

*Rabbi Israel
Zoberman
Virginia
Beach, Va.*

Tread carefully across
The threshold
Of a New Year,
Entering life's portals
Unhindered.
Gently leave the
Past behind,
Tucked under your
Bent figure.

Rabbi Israel Zoberman

The Irish Jewish Museum

Doctor Tolkin is on call at
Dublin's Irish Jewish Museum
In Little Jerusalem of old,
Presiding over those who landed
In Cork, believing they've arrived
At New York.
Pointing at the photo of Israel's
President Herzog, a native son,
With pride,
He counts the thousand souls
Of a remnant growing small,
Perhaps preserving those who
Enter the hallowed doors.

Rabbi Israel Zoberman

Migrant Ishmael

The migrant construction worker,
Attending to my synagogue,
Asked to fill a bucket with water.
And in his lowered eyes
I saw Ishmael begging
For sanctuary in the desert,
With Hagar's pleading voice
Disrupting the silence between us,
While Sarah's shadow was
Lurking behind stooped Abraham,
And Isaac –
Where were you brother?

The Pond At Birkenau

Rabbi Israel Zoberman

In winter's somberness
The pond at Birkenau
Submerged with human remains,
Contemplates the liberating spring
When blossoming flowers
Will bring to mind
What was plucked
Before its time,
That no snow
Could ever hide.

The Poet's Domain

Seasons & Crossroads

The POET'S DOMAIN

Acknowledges

The poem "The Desk" by Sharon Dorsey

as being selected as the

favored or best poem

by a majority of votes
from contributors to volume 33

Thank you to all who participated by their votes for the 1st Poet's Domain Contributor's Prize. The winner will receive a cash award and certificate, and will head the ranks of future winners of same...

The Poet's Domain

Meet the Poets of vol. 33 ...

Contact Points, Biographies, "Bios", Pointers, Accomplishments, Publications, Favorites, Discussion Points...

S.A. Borders-Shoemaker is a poet and fantasy and science-fiction author based in the Hampton Roads region of Virginia. She has two micronovels, The Conscious Objection, and Rooted In Time, along with numerous op-eds and a number of academic articles and nonfiction narratives. She recently earned her Ph.D. Her professional work as a Conflict Resolution practitioner specializes in interpersonal communication surrounding difficult subjects. When she's not writing, she spends her time with Tim, her husband, and their audacious corgi, Edmund.

Barbara Brady is a writer, poet and artist originally from Washington DC. Following a career in public health, she settled in the tidewater area of VA where her poetry and paintings are inspired by the natural landscapes and seascapes of the mid-Atlantic. Her poetry has been published in several regional and literary editions including *Pleasant Living Magazine* and volumes 14, 20, and 22 of *The Poet's Domain*.

Alisha Brown

Jason Brown (Published under the name Dark Matter)
Currently lives in Virginia Beach with his muse/fiancee Emily. Originally born in a concrete jungle but nurtured by the sea. The juxtaposition of his environments helps to create the time for almost all of Dark Matter's works. He currently has one book of poetry published, and another in the works. You can find more @Darkmtr across most social media outlets.

Jack Callan would rather die
        than write a bio -
                a-me-oh-my-oh.
He's got a notebook to lie through,
   and a tool bag to chisel his way out.
        (He ain't got no clout.)
He'd rather fly than mope about,
  but in these treasonous times,
        he is startin' to shout.

Joan Ellen Casey worked as an editor for New York publishers, trekked through South America alone as a female of twenty-five, raised a family, earned a doctorate from William & Mary, and wrote educational materials – then she quit to write poetry.

"The first poem I submitted for consideration won the Metrorail Public Art Project Award from the Poetry Society of Virginia. Since then I have been published in the last five volumes of *The Poet's Domain,* two other anthologies: *Distant Horizons* and *Captured Moments*, and have contributed to the Poetry Society of Virginia's Newsletter."

Norma Cofresi is a Clinical Psychologist, a Psychoanalyst, and writer. She was born in NYC to Puerto Rican parents and lived in New York City, Puerto Rico, and Cleveland, Ohio. She is happily married, has three adult children, and two grandchildren. Norma traded an apartment in the Bronx for a home in Williamsburg, Va. where she can sit in her backyard to commune with nature. She was reborn as a poet and fiction writer a year ago when she took a creative writing class with Janice Hoffman at Thomas Nelson Community College. Members of the James City County Poets Group provide guidance, friendship, and inspiration, for which she is grateful.
You can email her at Geminiris@icloud.com

Karen Cummings is an introvert with a good heart, a lil' sass, and spice for life! Born in California but raised in Virginia. she's a 33 yr. old half Black and Filipino woman who has a strong appreciation for her family. Growing up she was shy, but poetry was an outlet for her to express her thoughts and emotions without any restrictions.
Understanding the different layers of the human spirit is what interests her. Dr. Maya Angelou and Tupac Shakur were her inspirations growing up. She usually keeps to herself, but has decided to take a step outside of the comfort zone to share a few poems.

Sharon Canfield Dorsey has published fiction, non-fiction, juvenile fiction and poetry in magazines, newspapers, journals and anthologies. She is a member of National League of American Pen Women, Inc., and the James City Poets. She has received awards from Christopher Newport University Writer's Conference, Poetry Society of Virginia, Gulf Coast Writer's Association, and Chesapeake Bay Writers. She was a winner of the Art Lit Project, which displayed her poetry on the sidewalks of the city of Williamsburg, VA. Sharon is author of four children's books, *Herman, the Hermit Crab and the Mystery of the Big, Black, Shiny Thing; Revolt of the Teacups; Buddy and Ballerina Save the Library; Buddy the Bookworm Rescues the Doomed Books;* a book of poetry, *Tapestry;* a memoir, *Daughter of the Mountains,* and a travel memoir, *Road Trip*. Her poems are also included in an anthology, *Captured Moments*.

Anne Emerson is incorrigibly interested in everything. She likes to work with her hands, and also spends hours in thought - ideas running off in many directions. Her hobbies include writing poetry, taking photographs, gardening, knitting, crochet, and attempting to play the guitar. She currently has some creative ideas regarding why poverty can persist amid plenty, and what process in the brain causes psychosis.Born and raised in England, she met her husband at University, married him, and immigrated to the U.S. (7-7-'77). They lived in his native area, Washington DC, for forty-one years, and retired to Williamsburg, Va. in 2018. Her friend, Nannette Hoffman, taught her to write poetry as a form of therapy, after she experienced severe emotional distress at the age of thirty-nine. She learned spare use of words, and experimented with different forms and styles. In Reston, Va. Anne was active in two poetry workshops and a photography club. Anne took a number of different part-time jobs while her two children were growing up, notably as a photographer for Sears Portrait Studio, and an Economics teacher to working adults. When her children became more independent, she found full-time work as the back office mainstay of a technology start-up in Reston and participated in its growth to a mid-size company over fifteen years. Her poems have been published in *NOVA Bards*, and *the Poet's Domain*, for the past few years. She has self-published a book, Pics and Poems, of her photographs and poems, and has given presentations of poetry (her own and others') to senior communities in Reston and Williamsburg. Her latest project is an attempt at an academic paper, tentatively titled, "Divergent Income Paths: How Economic Growth Outruns Farmers and the Uneducated." Anne's address for any correspondence, is: PO Box 2623, Williamsburg, Virginia 23187.

Serena Fusek lives in Newport News with her husband where she is known as a somewhat eccentric cat lady. She has two full length collections of poetry: Alphabet of Foxes (San Francisco Bay Press) and Ancient Maps and a Tarot Pack which won the 2018 Bitter Oleander Press Library of Poetry Award. (She almost bought a Maine Coon Cat with the money but adopted a rescue tabby instead.) She teaches poetry at CNU's Life Long Learning Society and conducts workshops on various topics of poetic interest. Her hobby is amateur photography.

Amanda Gregory was born in Norfolk, VA and raised in Virginia Beach. She is a Life Doula who specializes in Sleep, Sex and Women's work. You can catch her sharing her light through different modalities such as freestyle spoken word, song, dance, women's empowerment events and traveling the world one country at a time. Amanda's purpose is to ignite the Wild Woman Within and to help you Break Free of limiting beliefs that have held you back from living your best life. Amanda published a poetry, picture book this year called Lights of Love. She has an adventurous soul and is all about LIVING LOVING LIFE. Follow her on FB Amanda Gregory Sleep or IG Sisterinshine33.

Linda Griffin

Doris Gwaltney is the author of four novels, Homefront, Shakespeare's Sister, Duncan Browdie, Gent., and Treason's Daughter.. She has also written two books of performance monologues which have been performed in many venues. She has had poetry and short fiction included in The Greensboro Review, In Good Company, William and Mary Review, The Poet's Domain, Virginia Adversaria, and other places.

George Barry Hamann of Poquoson usually appears in print as G. Barry

Jan Hoffman holds degrees from Indiana University; she teaches writing at the Historic Triangle Campus of Thomas Nelson Community College where she also co-hosts a monthly poetry reading. She is a member of the Poetry Society of Virginia for whom she edits *A Commonwealth of Poetry.* Her work appears in various literary journals and the anthologies of numerous state poetry societies; in 2017, she was runner-up for Poet Laureate of Hampton Roads. Her book of poetry, Soul Cookies (Hightide Publications), is followed soon by a children's book, Four Fairy Friends. In 2017, she was runner-up for Poet Laureate of Hampton Roads. Reach Jan at janhoffpoetry@gmail.com, on Facebook at janhoffpoetry, and at https://sites.google.com/view/janicehoffmanpoetry/home.

Shari Leigh is a native New Yorker whose collective life experiences have influences her creative processes. Spanning genres from comedy to poetry to abstract art, her work is illuminated by diversity and self-disclosure. Leigh currently lives in Norfolk, Va.

Terra Leigh is a poet, editor, and singer from Chesapeake, Va. She received her Bachelor's of Arts in English- Creative Writing from Virginia Tech, where she won the Stegler Poetry Prize. Then, she continued pursuing her love for writing and earned her Master's of Fine Arts in Poetry from Drew University, inspired by artists such as Maya Angelou and G Yamazawa. She has two poetry collections available, "Ignite" (2018) and "So Far Away" (2019), both published by Wider Perspectives Publishing. Outside of writing, reading, and editing, she loves to sing with her church's worship team and take sabre fencing lessons. If you're lucky, she might even speak a bit of Japanese to you, which she has been learning since 2011.

Edward W. Lull grew up in Upstate New York, and graduated from the U.S. Naval Academy in 1955. He earned a masters degree from The George Washington University in 1969. After retiring from the Navy in 1975, Lull held management and executive positions in several small hi-tech firms. He began writing poetry in retirement and has published 6 books of his poetry; he has also served four terms as President of The Poetry Society of Va.

Crickyt J. Expression Writing tools in her left hand so familiar that it feels naked without one, crayons the earliest favored, Crickyt has whispered to paper like it was a best friend all her life. In 2012, she stepped into the light of Hampton Roads open mics after a long stint of life in shadows. Finding a home and family at Norfolk's Venue on 35th, this Baltimore native was soon dubbed Little Mighty. Understanding one's voice is their most valuable asset, she uses her talents to encourage, comfort, and uplift others. Such is the focus of her new book Dear Broken Woman: Trials to Triumph.

Linda Partee As a California youngster, she wrote about everything she mused about, though never saved one scrap. Instead, her words were pushed through a hole in the wall that had been formed by too many hits of a doorknob and she's always wondered if her scraps were ever found. Linda earned her college degrees at California State University, Fullerton; a B.A. in Communications and her M.A. in Speech & Language Pathology. During a 3-decade career in education and administration, she was called upon to focus her writing skills toward technical, educational and government requirements. The joy of words began to dissolve. In retirement, she moved cross-country to

Williamsburg, enrolled in her first Christopher Wren writing class, and lovely words came flooding back. This time, she saved them. Linda began to dabble with poetry, and really likes to write in form. She is a member of the James City Poets, The Williamsburg Poetry Guild and Chesapeake Bay Writers. During the coldest months, you can find her teaching poetry through the Osher Lifelong Learning Institute at the College of William and Mary.

Lucy Quinn; Born in Michigan, Lucy came to Virginia in 2010 as a mobilized Navy Reservist, Public Affairs Officer. As a civilian she worked in publishing and corporate communications as a writer and editor. After making Virginia her home she retired from the Navy and works now as a freelance writer and poet.

Robert Rickard is a retired federal executive who lives and writes on Capital Hill, in Washington DC, and at *Laetare,* his waterfront haven in the Northern Neck of Virginia. His poetry appeared in the Poetry Society of Virginia's 80th Anniversary Anthology of Poems, *2003;* in *Pleasant Living Magazine;* and in 13 volumes of *The Poet's Domain.* His Book, Until the Singing Ends, was published in 2019 by Live Wire Press.

Dawn Riddle, a Virginia native, was born along with her identical twin in 1967. She earned degrees in Sociology at Virginia colleges: Mary Washington and William & Mary, respectively. Riddle has managed the restored Victorian 1889 *Mansion on Main* in Smithfield's Historic District for over 15 years. She leads the *Isle of Wight Writers Group* with its beloved matriarch, Doris Gwaltney. Multiple poems have been exhibited at Smithfield's Arts Center/"Arts@319" with co-sponsored themed events. Riddle has been published in recent editions of *The Poet's Domain* by Live Wire Press.

Kailyn Sasso Born and raised in Grand Rapids, Michigan, Kailyn Sasso is a northern girl at heart; considering a majority of her inspiration is drawn from her fellow Michiganders. The Crane Wives, La Dispute, and WYCE's Electric Poetry have pushed her to explore all realms of writing over the years. Her poetry has strong Dorothy Parker mixed with Rupi Kaur vibes, leaving you melancholy yet grounded at the same time. Since moving to Virginia, she's become enamored with Norfolk's poetry scene. She often performs at open mic nights and is currently working on publishing a poetic memoir with Wider Perspectives.

Ann Shalaski was born and raised in Connecticut and spent her formative years nurtured by a warm, loving and, at times, loud Italian family. Much of her work delves into those vivid memories. She is an award-winning poet whose pieces have appeared in numerous journals and anthologies. Her story of a family's disconnect and rivalry appears in Keeper of the Stories, a Guide to Writing Family Stories. She is the author of three poetry collections, the last of which was Just So You Know from Live Wire Press. Ann is a member of National League of American Pen Women. She is a former officer with the Poetry Society of Virginia. She hosts a monthly poetry open mic in Newport News.

Barbara Drucker Smith is a regional and national anthologized poet, non-fiction and fiction writer. She is author of Darling Lorraine, the story of A. Louis Drucker, A Grateful Jewish Immigrant – Poetic Journey, nominated for the Library of Virginia Awards. She is owner-operator of Louraine Publishing. She is a certified English, Speech, & Journalism teacher and taught at Ferguson High School. She's a member of Tidewater Writer's Assoc., VA Writers, Poetry Society of VA, SHARP Society of Historians, and has worked in blown glass, composing and piano, swimming and travelling the world.

Karen Sparrow hails from Buckroe Beach. She wrote her first poem when she was in JR. High School. "Fortunately, none of my early stuff survived." She has two children. Her daughter is her biggest fan. She's had poems published in the *Poquoson Historical Commission Newsletter*, Poquoson Library's Teen Advisory Board's poetry contest books and has won third place. She has poems in anthologies Your Virginia and Forever in Our Hearts. She has also had poems hung on the walls of the Charles H. Taylor art center. Karen enjoys reading, writing, going to open mics and being with friends and family.

Judith Stevens has been a writer since the second grade, and she finds inspiration in the woods and mountains, in her poet-husband, Jack Callan, in the sonnets of Edna St.Vincent Millay, and in the heroism of so-called "ordinary people." Her poems often highlight issues of social justice and tell stories, true and embellished. Co-creator with her husband of "The Little River Poetry Festival," held each June in the Blue Ridge Mountain town of Floyd, Virginia, she can often be found leading yoga and meditation in the Festival tent, hiking up Rocky Knob, or floating down the Little River in a kayak, writing poems. Her work has been published by the Helen Keller Foundation, *Venture Inward* magazine, the *A.R.E. Journal*, *The New Millennium*, *Randolph-Macon Men's College Literary Journal* and *The Piedmont Literary Review.*

Ken Sutton is not crazy. But he does have voices in his head, old men and children, friends and enemies, close relatives and people who waited with him at a bus stop in 1966. They have something to say, an act to justify, a sorrow to share, a moment of awe that overcame them in the event and still does in memory. He has two books out, Manhattan to Machipongo and The Convenience of War. He will be bringing The Midrash of the Marginal out soon and Water from a Bitter Well is nearing completion.
Letters of adoration may be sent to P. O. Box 81, Machipongo VA 23405.

Tammy Tillotson lives in Chase City, Virginia. Her chapbook Lady Fingers was published by Finishing Line Press in 2012. Her award-winning poems, fiction and nonfiction have been published in various print and online publications. She is a member of the Poetry Society of Virginia, the Writers Studio in South Boston, and often reads at WAM Poetry Nights in Warrenton, NC. She holds a Master of Arts in Liberal Studies from Hollins University & is active in community theater, currently serving on its Board of Directors. When not attending meetings that could've been emails, she carpools kids to every activity under the sun while somehow managing to keep up the pretty good act of being a domestic engineer.

12 Keys; Catherine Teresa Lane Hodges, aka Kittee, aka 12 Keys began poetry after a very profound meeting with Maya Angelou at the age of seven. Her writing is a combination of folk (as it tells a story) and proverbs (as it teaches a lesson). The recent loss of her mother made her want to put down her pen indefinitely, but her mother was one of her biggest fans, and she never wanted to disappoint her. Kittee's current mission is to write through the pain!

Jack Underhill has a PhD. From George Mason University in public policy and an MA in public administration from Harvard's Kennedy School of Government along with degrees from UC Berkeley and

Columbia. He retired in 1997 after forty-two years in Federal service. He participates in the poetry workshop at GMU's Osher Lifelong Learning Center, in the PSV as a former VP, and in previous volumes of The Poet's Domain.

Charles Wilson is a poet, artist, and musician. Originally from Macon, Georgia, he served 26 years in the U.S. Navy. A Pushcart Prize nominee, he has published his poems and art in such journals as Sow's Ear Poetry Review, Four Ties Literary Review, The Blue Hour, 100 Word Story, and TEXTure Magazine. He resides in Virginia Beach with his collection of guitars and mandolins.

J. Scott Wilson is an opaque surfaced, three-dimensional being who participates in heterotrophoism, heterosexuality and heterodontia. He has been published in The Poet's Domain and then helped to create the Hampton Roads Artistic Collective and Wider Perspectives Publishing. Much of his poetry expresses concern over social justice and how we, as humans, treat each other. He invites discussion at any of the many open mics he goes to all around Virginia, where he takes the stage under the name "TEECH!"

Henriann Woleben was born in Bay City Michigan, but has been a resident of Virginia since early childhood. She is a graduate of Westhampton College – University of Richmond. She has a lifelong love of books, art and writing. She retired after 38 years of teaching English and Library Instruction at Nansemond Suffolk Academy. Gardening allows her time to meditate and relax and provides much inspiration for her poetry and artwork.

Gus M. Woodward II is a loving old soul with a young spirit born and raised in Virginia Beach. A 31 year old father and just getting started on discovering his purpose; To spread unconditional love through any and every method or medium, any interaction or conversation. He was raised by a father that taught me how to practice the art of happiness and a mother that opened up the world of creative expression at a very young age. Now as a father, his whole day rises and sets around my son. Though given a number of stage names like G2, MC Gusto, Gustarhymez he is simply Gus and poetry is his true language.

Rabbi Dr. Israel Zoberman is the founder and spiritual leader of Temple Lev Tikvah in Virginia Beach, Virginia. He was born in 1945 in Chu, Kazakhstan (USSR) to Polish Holocaust survivors. He spent his early childhood in Poland, Austria and Germany before moving to Israel in 1949. He came to Chicago in 1966. His poetry and translations from Hebrew have been published in *CCAR Journal*, *Poetica*, *The Jewish Spectator*, *The American Rabbi, Moment*, and [The Poet's Domain](), Volumes 5 through 33.

Editor's Rambling Thoughts
or
Foreword That Got Put in the Back

The original intent of these passages were to go up front, but a more important announcement superseded.

I am driving by the root of Cromwell Ave in Norfolk and pass a spot that I have passed hundreds of times since learning to drive, and hundreds of times before. It is a double storefront at the end of a not-always successful strip shopping center that has been around since way before my time. I keep waiting for it to reopen as a doctor's office, though nothing has occupied that particular shop for easily twenty years. The shops facing Tidewater Drive seem to found a certain stability, but these sloping away and then facing Cromwell seem to hang on by a thread, or fall off.

For the half of my life that is dominated by my pre-driving era that shop front was occupied by the office of doctors Lerner and Krueger, my family's physicians of choice from before my birth right into my teens. I continued to see them for medical needs well into the time my nuclear-most family lived in Hampton. I think we only stopped going with the appearance of doc-in-the-box, which made trans-harbor drives for medical attention into an unnecessary expense in money and time.

That office, however, is what I keep waiting for to reappear. There has even been an intervening business – a short-lived wig and beauty shop – in that space. Nope,… it is the doctor's office of my youth that goes there and I constantly await it's return. I didn't even like visits to the doctor, nor even the doctors themselves, which I told them over MMR & DipTet cocktails. But I realize that it's probably because I don't usually have seasons and I seldom capitalize on crossroads. Things and places and paths are often assumed as permanent in my mind, perhaps irrationally, perhaps to absurdity.

My first thought on changing with seasons, going with flows, rolling with tides is one of impermanence, transience, or perhaps even frailty. Apparently it is easy for me to forget that flexibility is a strength in it's own right. I see the mighty oaks fighting the hurricanes, but I forget the willow has a strategy that is as successful, or even moreso.

And of crossroads I might think they serve to distract, and therefore waylay those on a mission. However they often represent options, better destinies and unforeseen opportunities, or at least a shortcut to the same original destination.

Potential for good and bad lay in both changing seasons and taking crossroads, a lesson I relearn frequently and forget as often. Staying in a relationship for the sake of a remembered temperate Spring and hoping for its return while the Autumn blusters with the threat of a season of freeze – and of die … well that's wishful thinking against evidence to the contrary. Good luck with that. Yes, I do mean to make myself sound a bit foolhardy … er, I mean such a person. Well, permanence was the objective anyways, but should it have been? Seasonless, unwavering me never questioned until the abuses heaped upon abuses became difficult to see over.

Even here, close to home, I proceed with this venture, but at my feet lays a crossing path. The partner who helped me walk into this business stepped back to concentrate on other parts of her life; family, career,… family. She has a set of crossroads of her own to venture down. Perhaps publishing was simply a season for her. With open invitation to return to the game anytime, picking up where she left off, she gets to do the other thing crossroads maybe hopefully offer – a chance to roll on down a ways and then come back to where you turned off.

Carrying on with the chosen path welcome to The Poet's Domain: vol.33   Seasons and Crossroads